Canadian
Political Facts 1945–1976

Methuen: Canadian Politics and Government

Canadian Political Facts 1945–1976

Colin Campbell

Mount Allison University

Methuen
Toronto • London • New York • Sydney

Canadian Cataloguing in Publication Data

Campbell, Colin, 1944-
Canadian political facts, 1945-1976

ISBN 0-458-92660-4 bd. ISBN 0-458-92430-X pa.

1. Canada — Politics and government — 1935-
— Handbooks, manuals, etc.* I. Title.

JL78 1977.C34   320.9′71′064   C77-001204-3

Printed and bound in Canada

1 2 3 4 5   81 80 79 78 77

Contents

Acknowledgements

I would like to acknowledge the assistance given to me by Mount Allison University through the Humanities and Social Science Research Fund, which enabled me to obtain the services of my able research assistant, Don C. Murray. The staff of the Ralph Pickard Bell Memorial Library has, as usual, been most helpful. Last, but by no means least, I must thank my efficient and hard-working secretary, Miss Louise Smith.

I
THE EXECUTIVE

1. Sovereign

George VI	11 Dec 1936 – 6 Feb 1952
Elizabeth II	6 Feb 1952 –

2. Governor General and Commander-in-Chief

	Date of Appointment
Earl of Athlone	3 Apr 1940
Viscount Alexander	21 Mar 1946
Vincent Massey	24 Jan 1952
General Georges Vanier	1 Aug 1959
Roland Michener	29 Mar 1967
Jules Léger	5 Oct 1973

Source: *Canada Year Book 1974.*

3. Canadian Ministries 1945-1976

This section lists those who have held office in Canadian ministries since January 1, 1945. It is subdivided at each change of Prime Minister and within each subdivision the holders of ministerial office are given chronologically. In the event that an office was abolished or reorganized during the life of a ministry, the list of ministers ends at the relevant date without further note. A vacant but still existing office is designated as vacant and the dates of vacancy are specified.

The next section (Ministers by Department 1945–1976) cross-indexes this information by providing a continuous list of office holders for each ministerial position since 1945. The abolition or reorganization of an office is indicated. In both sections the entry 1945 indicates that the person named held office on January 1, 1945.

Sources: *Guide to Canadian Ministries Since Confederation July 1, 1867* – April 1, 1973, Ottawa: Public Archives of Canada, 1974; *Canada Year Book, 1974* – .

King Government (Liberal) 1945–1948

Prime Minister
W.L.M. King	1945 – 15 Nov 1948

President of the Privy Council
W.L.M. King	1945 – 15 Nov 1948

Secretary of State for External Affairs
W.L.M. King	1945 – 3 Sep 1946
L.S. St. Laurent	4 Sep 1946 – 9 Sep 1948
L.B. Pearson	10 Sep 1948 – 15 Nov 1948

Minister of Mines and Resources
T.A. Crerar   1945 – 17 Apr 1945
J.A. Glen   18 Apr 1945 – 10 Jun 1948
J.A. MacKinnon   11 Jun 1948 – 15 Nov 1948

Minister of Justice and Attorney General
L.S. St. Laurent   1945 – 9 Dec 1946
J.L. Ilsley   10 Dec 1946 – 30 Jun 1948
L.S. St. Laurent (Acting)   1 Jul 1948 – 9 Sep 1948
L.S. St. Laurent   10 Sep 1948 – 15 Nov 1948

Minister of Public Works
A. Fournier   1945 – 15 Nov 1948

Minister of Finance and Receiver General
J.L. Ilsley   1945 – 9 Dec 1946
D.C. Abbott   10 Dec 1946 – 15 Nov 1948

Postmaster General
W.P. Mulock   1945 – 8 Jun 1945
Vacant   9 Jun 1945 – 28 Aug 1945
E. Bertrand   29 Aug 1945 – 14 Nov 1948

Minister of Trade and Commerce
J.A. MacKinnon   1945 – 18 Jan 1948
C.D. Howe   19 Jan 1948 – 15 Nov 1948

Secretary of State of Canada
N.A. McLarty   15 Dec 1945 – 17 Apr 1945
P.J.J. Martin   18 Apr 1945 – 11 Dec 1946
C.W.G. Gibson   12 Dec 1946 – 15 Nov 1948

Minister of National Defence
A.G.L. McNaughton   1945 – 20 Aug 1945
D.C. Abbott   21 Aug 1945 – 11 Dec 1946
B. Claxton   12 Dec 1946 – 15 Nov 1948

Minister of National Defence for Air
A.L. Macdonald (Acting)   1945 – 10 Jan 1945
C.W.G. Gibson (Acting)   11 Jan 1945 – 7 Mar 1945
C.W.G. Gibson   8 Mar 1945 – 11 Dec 1945

Minister of National Defence for Naval Services
A.L. Macdonald   1945 – 17 Apr 1945
D.C. Abbott   18 Apr 1945 – 11 Dec 1946

Minister of Veterans' Affairs
I.A. Mackenzie   1945 – 18 Jan 1948
M.F. Gregg   19 Jan 1948 – 15 Nov 1948

Minister of National Health and Welfare
B. Claxton   1945–11 Dec 1946
P.J.J. Martin   12 Dec 1946–15 Nov 1948

Minister of National Revenue
C.W.G. Gibson   1945–7 Mar 1945
J.A. MacKinnon (Acting)   8 Mar 1945–18 Apr 1945
D.L. MacLaren   19 Apr 1945–29 Jul 1945
J.A. MacKinnon (Acting)   30 Jul 1945–28 Aug 1945
J.J. McCann   29 Aug 1945–15 Nov 1948

Minister of Fisheries
E. Bertrand   1945–28 Aug 1945
H.F.G. Bridges   29 Aug 1945–10 Aug 1947
Vacant   11 Aug 1947–13 Aug 1947
E. Bertrand (Acting)   14 Aug 1947–1 Sep 1947
M.F. Gregg   2 Sep 1947–18 Jan 1948
J.A. MacKinnon   19 Jan 1948–10 Jun 1948
R.W. Mayhew   11 Jun 1948–15 Nov 1948

Minister of Labour
H. Mitchell   1945–15 Nov 1948

Minister of Transport
J.E. Michaud   1945–17 Apr 1945
L. Chevrier   18 Apr 1945–15 Nov 1948

Minister of Munitions and Supply
C.D. Howe   1945–31 Dec 1945

Minister of Reconstruction
C.D. Howe   1945–31 Dec 1945

Minister of Reconstruction and Supply
C.D. Howe   1 Jan 1946–15 Nov 1948

Minister of Agriculture
J.G. Gardiner   1945–15 Nov 1948

Solicitor General
Vacant   1945–17 Apr 1945
J. Jean   18 Apr 1945–15 Nov 1948

Minister of National War Services
L.R. Laflèche   1945–17 Apr 1945
J.J. McCann   18 Apr 1945–18 Jan 1948
Vacant   19 Jan 1948–15 Nov 1948

Member of the Administration and Minister Without Portfolio
J.H. King (Leaders of
Government in Senate)   1945–23 Aug 1945
W.M. Robertson (Leader
of Government in Senate)   4 Sep 1945–15 Nov 1948

St. Laurent Government (Liberal) 1948–1957

Prime Minister
L.S. St. Laurent   15 Nov 1948–21 Jun 1957

President of the Privy Council
L.S. St. Laurent   15 Nov 1948–24 Apr 1957
L. Chevrier   25 Apr 1957–21 Jun 1957

Minister of Trade and Commerce
C.D. Howe   15 Nov 1948–21 Jun 1957

Minister of Agriculture
J.G. Gardiner   15 Nov 1948–21 Jun 1957

Minister of Mines and Resources
J.A. MacKinnon   15 Nov 1948–31 Mar 1949
C.W.G. Gibson   1 Apr 1949–17 Jan 1950

Secretary of State of Canada
C.W.G. Gibson   15 Nov 1948–31 Mar 1949
F.G. Bradley   1 Apr 1949–11 Jun 1953
J.W. Pickersgill   12 Jun 1953–30 Jun 1954
R. Pinard   1 Jul 1954–21 Jun 1957

Minister of Labour
H. Mitchell   15 Nov 1948–2 Aug 1950
P.J.J. Martin (Acting)   3 Aug 1950–6 Aug 1950
M.F. Gregg   7 Aug 1950–21 Jun 1957

Minister of Public Works
A. Fournier   15 Nov 1948–11 Jun 1953
W.E. Harris (Acting)   12 Jun 1953–16 Sep 1953
R.H. Winters   17 Sep 1953–21 Jun 1957

Postmaster General
E. Bertrand   15 Nov 1948–23 Aug 1949
Vacant   24 Aug 1949
G.E. Rinfret   25 Aug 1949–12 Feb 1952
A. Côté   13 Feb 1952–7 Aug 1955
Vacant   8 Aug 1955–15 Aug 1955
R. Pinard (Acting)   16 Aug 1955–2 Nov 1955

H. Lapointe   3 Nov 1955–21 Jun 1957

Minister of National Defence
B. Claxton   15 Nov 1948–30 Jun 1954
R.O. Campney   1 Jul 1954–21 Jun 1957

Associate Minister of National Defence
Vacant   11 Feb 1953
R.O. Campney   12 Feb 1953–30 Jun 1954
Vacant   1 July 1954–25 Apr 1957
P.T. Hellyer   26 Apr 1957–21 Jun 1957

Solicitor General
J. Jean   15 Nov 1948–23 Aug 1949
H. Lapointe   24 Aug 1949–6 Aug 1950
S.S. Garson   7 Aug 1950–14 Oct 1952
R.O. Campney   15 Oct 1952–11 Jan 1954
*W.R. Macdonald   12 Jan 1954–21 Jun 1957
*Also Leader of Government in Senate.

Minister of Transport
L. Chevrier   15 Nov 1948–30 Jun 1954
G.C. Marler   1 Jul 1954–21 Jun 1957

Minister of National Health and Welfare
P.J.J. Martin   15 Nov 1948–21 Jun 1957

Minister of Finance and Receiver General
D.C. Abbott   15 Nov 1948–30 Jun 1954
W.E. Harris   1 Jul 1954–21 Jun 1957

Minister of National Revenue
J.J. McCann   15 Nov 1948–21 Jun 1957

Minister of Veterans' Affairs
M.F. Gregg   15 Nov 1948–6 Aug 1950
H. Lapointe   7 Aug 1950–21 Jun 1957

Minister of Fisheries
R.W. Mayhew   15 Nov 1948–14 Oct 1952
J. Sinclair   15 Oct 1952–21 Jun 1957

Secretary of State for External Affairs
L.B. Pearson   15 Nov 1948–21 Jun 1957

Minister of Justice and Attorney General
S.S. Garson   15 Nov 1948–21 Jun 1957

Minister of Reconstruction and Supply
R.H. Winters   15 Nov 1948–17 Jan 1950

Minister of Resources and Development
R.H. Winters   18 Jan 1950—16 Sep 1953
J. Lesage   17 Sep 1953—15 Dec 1953

Minister of Northern Affairs and National Resources
J. Lesage   16 Dec 1953—21 Jun 1957

Member of the Administration and Minister Without Portfolio
W.M. Robertson (Leader   15 Nov 1948—13 Oct 1953
of Government in Senate)
J.A. MacKinnon   1 Apr 1949—13 Dec 1950
W.R. Macdonald (Leader   14 Oct 1953—11 Jan 1954
of Government in Senate)

Minister of Mines and Technical Surveys
J.J. McCann   18 Jan 1950—12 Dec 1950
G. Prudham   13 Jan 1950—21 Jun 1957

Minister of Citizenship and Immigration
W.E. Harris   18 Jan 1950—30 Jun 1954
J.W. Pickersgill   1 Jul 1954—21 Jun 1957

Minister of Defence Production
C.D. Howe   1 Apr 1951—21 Jun 1957

Diefenbaker Government (Conservative) 1957—1963

Prime Minister
J.G. Diefenbaker   21 Jun 1957—22 Apr 1963

President of the Privy Council
Vacant   21 Jun 1957—27 Dec 1961
N. Dorion   28 Dec 1961—5 Jul 1962
Vacant   6 Jul 1962—20 Dec 1962
J.G. Diefenbaker   21 Dec 1962—22 Apr 1963

Secretary of State for External Affairs
J.G. Diefenbaker   21 Jun 1957—12 Sep 1957
S.E. Smith   13 Sep 1957—17 Mar 1959
Vacant   18 Mar 1959
J.G. Diefenbaker (Acting)   19 Mar 1959—3 Jun 1959
H.C. Green   4 Jun 1959—22 Apr 1963

Minister of Public Works
H.C. Green   21 Jun 1957—19 Aug 1959
D.J. Walker   20 Aug 1959—12 Jul 1962
Vacant   13 Jul 1962—17 Jul 1962
H.C. Green (Acting)   18 Jul 1962—8 Aug 1962
E.D. Fulton   9 Aug 1962—22 Apr 1963

Minister of Finance and Receiver General
D.M. Fleming	21 Jun 1957–8 Aug 1962
G.C. Nowlan	9 Aug 1962–22 Apr 1963

Minister of Veterans' Affairs
A.J. Brooks	21 Jun 1957–10 Oct 1960
G. Churchill	11 Oct 1960–11 Feb 1963
M.J.A. Lambert	12 Feb 1963–22 Apr 1963

Solicitor General
L. Balcer	21 Jun 1957–10 Oct 1960
W.J. Browne	11 Oct 1960–9 Aug 1962
Vacant	10 Aug 1962–22 Apr 1963

Minister of Transport
G. Hees	21 Jun 1957–10 Oct 1960
L. Balcer	11 Oct 1960–22 Apr 1963

Minister of National Defence
G.R. Pearkes	21 Jun 1957–10 Oct 1960
D.S. Harkness	11 Oct 1960–3 Feb 1963
Vacant	4 Feb 1963–11 Feb 1963
G. Churchill	12 Feb 1963–22 Apr 1963

Minister of Trade and Commerce
G. Churchill	21 Jun 1957–10 Oct 1960
G. Hees	11 Oct 1960–8 Feb 1963
Vacant	9 Feb 1963–11 Feb 1963
M.W. McCutcheon (Senator)	12 Feb 1963–22 Apr 1963

Minister of Justice and Attorney General
E.D. Fulton	21 Jun 1957–8 Aug 1962
D.M. Fleming	9 Aug 1962–22 Apr 1963

Minister of National Revenue
G.C. Nowlan	21 Jun 1957–8 Aug 1962
H.J. Flemming	9 Aug 1962–22 Apr 1963

Minister of Northern Affairs and National Resources
D.S. Harkness	21 Jun 1957–18 Aug 1957
Vacant	19 Aug 1957–21 Aug 1957
F.A.G. Hamilton	22 Aug 1957–10 Oct 1960
W.G. Dinsdale	11 Oct 1960–22 Apr 1963

Secretary of State of Canada
E.L. Fairclough	21 Jun 1957–11 May 1958
H. Courtemanche	12 May 1958–19 Jan 1960
Vacant	20 Jan 1960
L. Balcer (Acting)	21 Jan 1960–10 Oct 1960

N. Dorion	11 Oct 1960–5 Jul 1962
Vacant	6 Jul 1962–10 Jul 1962
L. Balcer (Acting)	11 Jul 1962–8 Aug 1962
G.E. Halpenny	9 Aug 1962–22 Apr 1963

Minister of Fisheries

J.A. MacLean	21 Jun 1957–22 Apr 1963

Minister of Labour

M. Starr	21 Jun 1957–22 Apr 1963

Postmaster General

W.M. Hamilton	21 Jun 1957–12 Jul 1962
Vacant	13 Jul 1962–17 Jul 1962
J.A. MacLean (Acting)	18 Jul 1962–8 Aug 1962
E.L. Fairclough	9 Aug 1962–22 Apr 1963

Minister of Agriculture

D.S. Harkness (Acting)	21 Jun 1957–6 Aug 1957
D.S. Harkness	7 Aug 1957–10 Oct 1960
F.A.G. Hamilton	11 Oct 1960–22 Apr 1963

Minister of Mines and Technical Surveys

L. Balcer (Acting)	21 Jun 1957–6 Aug 1957
P. Comtois	7 Aug 1957–6 Oct 1961
Vacant	7 Oct 1961–9 Oct 1961
W.G. Dinsdale (Acting)	10 Oct 1961–27 Dec 1961
J. Flynn	28 Dec 1961–12 Jul 1962
Vacant	13 Jul 1962–17 Jul 1962
H.J. Flemming (Acting)	18 Jul 1962–8 Aug 1962
P. Martineau	9 Aug 1962–22 Apr 1963

Minister of National Health and Welfare

A.J. Brooks (Acting)	21 Jun 1957–21 Aug 1957
J.W. Monteith	22 Aug 1957–22 Apr 1963

Minister of Citizenship and Immigration

E.D. Fulton (Acting)	21 Jun 1957–11 May 1958
E.L. Fairclough	12 May 1958–8 Aug 1962
R.A. Bell	9 Aug 1962–22 Apr 1963

Minister of Defence Production

H.C. Green (Acting)	21 Jun 1957–11 May 1958
R.J.M. O'Hurley	12 May 1958–22 Apr 1963

Associate Minister of National Defence

Vacant	21 Jun 1957–19 Aug 1959
J.P.A. Sévigny	20 Aug 1959–8 Feb 1963
Vacant	9 Feb 1963–22 Apr 1963

Minister of Forestry

Vacant	1 Oct 1960–10 Oct 1960
H.J. Flemming	11 Oct 1960–17 Mar 1963
M. Asselin	18 Mar 1963–22 Apr 1963

Member of the Administration and Minister Without Portfolio

J.M. Macdonnell	21 Jun 1957–19 Aug 1959
W.J. Browne	21 Jun 1957–10 Oct 1960
J.T. Haig	9 Oct 1957–11 May 1958
G.E. Halpenny	11 Oct 1960–8 Aug 1962
M.W. McCutcheon	9 Aug 1962–11 Feb 1963
T. Ricard	18 Mar 1963–22 Apr 1963
F.C. McGee	18 Mar 1963–22 Apr 1963

Pearson Government (Liberal) 1963–1968

Prime Minister

L.B. Pearson	22 Apr 1963–20 Apr 1968

Minister of Justice and Attorney General

L. Chevrier	22 Apr 1963–2 Feb 1964
G. Favreau	3 Feb 1964–29 Jun 1965
G.J. McIlraith (Acting)	30 Jun 1965–6 Jul 1965
L. Cardin	7 Jul 1965–3 Apr 1967
P.E. Trudeau	4 Apr 1967–20 Apr 1968

Secretary of State for External Affairs

P.J.J. Martin	22 Apr 1963–20 Apr 1968

Secretary of State for Canada

J.W. Pickersgill	22 Apr 1963–2 Feb 1964
M. Lamontagne	3 Feb 1964–17 Dec 1965
J.V. LaMarsh	18 Dec 1965–9 Apr 1968
J.J. Connolly (Acting)	10 Apr 1968–20 Apr 1968

Minister of National Defence

P.T. Hellyer	22 Apr 1963–18 Sep 1967
L.A.J. Cadieux	19 Sep 1967–20 Apr 1968

Associate Minister of National Defence

L. Cardin	22 Apr 1963–14 Feb 1965
L.A.J. Cadieux	15 Feb 1965–18 Sep 1967
Vacant	19 Sep 1967–20 Apr 1968

Minister of National Revenue

J.R. Garland	22 Apr 1963–14 Mar 1964
Vacant	15 Mar 1964–18 Mar 1964
G.J. McIlraith (Acting)	19 Mar 1964–28 Jun 1964
E. Benson	29 Jun 1964–17 Jan 1968

J. Chrétien   18 Jan 1968–20 Apr 1968

Minister of Labour
A.J. MacEachen   22 Apr 1963–17 Dec 1965
J.R. Nicholson   18 Dec 1965–20 Apr 1968

Minister of Public Works
J.P. Deschatelets   22 Apr 1963–11 Feb 1965
Vacant   12 Feb 1965–14 Feb 1965
L. Cardin   15 Feb 1965–6 Jul 1965
G.J. McIlraith   7 Jul 1965–20 Apr 1968

Minister of Fisheries
H. Robichaud   22 Apr 1963–20 Apr 1968

Solicitor General
J.W. MacNaught   22 Apr 1963–6 Jul 1965
L.T. Pennell   7 Jul 1965–19 Apr 1968

Minister of Veterans' Affairs
R.J. Teillet   22 Apr 1963–20 Apr 1968

Minister of National Health and Welfare
J.V. LaMarsh   22 Apr 1963–17 Dec 1965
A.J. MacEachen   18 Dec 1965–20 Apr 1968

Minister of Defence Production
C.M. Drury   22 Apr 1963–20 Apr 1968

Minister of Industry
C.M. Drury   25 Jul 1963–20 Apr 1968

Minister of Citizenship and Immigration
G. Favreau   22 Apr 1963–2 Feb 1964
R. Tremblay   3 Feb 1964–14 Feb 1965
J.R. Nicholson   15 Feb 1965–17 Dec 1965
J. Marchand   18 Dec 1965–30 Sep 1966

Minister of Manpower and Immigration
J. Marchand   1 Oct 1966–20 Apr 1968

Minister of Finance and Receiver General
W.L. Gordon   22 Apr 1963–10 Nov 1965
M.W. Sharp (Acting)   11 Nov 1965–17 Dec 1965
M.W. Sharp   18 Dec 1965–20 Apr 1968

Minister of Trade and Commerce
M.W. Sharp   22 Apr 1963–3 Jan 1966
R.H. Winters   4 Jan 1966–29 Mar 1968
J.-L. Pepin   30 Mar 1968–20 Apr 1968

Postmaster General
A. Denis	22 Apr 1963–2 Feb 1964
J.R. Nicholson	3 Feb 1964–14 Feb 1965
R. Tremblay	15 Feb 1965–17 Dec 1965
J.-P. Côté	18 Dec 1965–20 Apr 1968

Minister of Transport
G.J. McIlraith	22 Apr 1963–2 Feb 1964
J.W. Pickersgill	3 Feb 1964–18 Sep 1967
P.T. Hellyer	19 Sep 1967–20 Apr 1968

Minister of Mines and Technical Surveys
W.M. Benidickson	22 Apr 1963–6 Jul 1965
J.W. MacNaught	7 Jul 1965–17 Dec 1965
J.-L. Pepin	18 Dec 1965–30 Sep 1966

Minister of Energy, Mines and Resources
J.-L. Pepin	1 Oct 1966–20 Apr 1968

Minister of Northern Affairs and National Resources
A. Laing	22 Apr 1963–30 Sep 1966

Minister of Indian Affairs and Northern Development
A. Laing	1 Oct 1966–20 Apr 1968

President of the Privy Council
M. Lamontagne	22 Apr 1963–2 Feb 1964
G.J. McIlraith	3 Feb 1964–6 Jul 1965
G. Favreau	7 Jul 1965–3 Apr 1967
W.L. Gordon	4 Apr 1967–10 Mar 1968
P.E. Trudeau (Acting)	11 Mar 1968–20 Apr 1968

Minister of Forestry
J.R. Nicholson	22 Apr 1963–2 Feb 1964
M. Sauvé	3 Feb 1964–30 Sep 1966

Minister of Forestry and Rural Development
M. Sauvé	1 Oct 1966–20 Apr 1968

Minister of Agriculture
H.W. Hays	22 Apr 1963–17 Dec 1965
J.J. Greene	18 Dec 1965–20 Apr 1968

Member of the Administration and Minister Without Portfolio
W.R. Macdonald (Leader of Government in Senate)	22 Apr 1963–2 Feb 1964
R. Tremblay	22 Apr. 1963–2 Feb 1964
J.W. MacNaught	22 Apr 1963–6 Jul 1965

J.J. Connolly (Leader
of Government in Senate)   3 Feb 1964–20 Apr 1968
Y. Dupuis   3 Feb 1964–21 Jan 1965
J.-L. Pepin   7 Jul 1965–17 Dec 1965
L.T. Pennell   7 Jul 1965–30 Sep 1966
J.N. Turner   18 Dec 1965–3 Apr 1967
W.L. Gordon   9 Jan 1967–3 Apr 1967
J. Chrétien   4 Apr 1967–17 Jan 1968
C.R.M. Granger   25 Sep 1967–20 Apr 1968
B.S. Mackasey   9 Feb 1968–20 Apr 1968

President of the Treasury Board
E. Benson   1 Oct 1966–20 Apr 1968

Minister of Consumer and Corporate Affairs
J.N. Turner   10 Jan 1968–20 Apr 1968

Registrar General of Canada
G. Favreau   1 Oct 1966–3Apr 1967
J.N. Turner   4 Apr 1967–20 Dec 1967

Trudeau Government (Liberal) 1968–

Prime Minister
P.E. Trudeau   20 Apr 1968–

Minister of Transport
P.T. Hellyer   20 Apr 1968–29 Apr 1969
J.A. Richardson (Acting)   30 Apr 1969–4 May 1969
D.C. Jamieson   5 May 1969–26 Nov 1972
J. Marchand   27 Nov 1972–25 Sep 1975
O.E. Lang   26 Sep 1975–

Secretary of State for External Affairs
M.W. Sharp   20 Apr 1968–7 Aug 1974
A.J. MacEachen   8 Aug 1974–14 Sep 1976
D.C. Jamieson   15 Sep 1976–

Solicitor General
J.N. Turner   20 Apr 1968–5 Jul 1968
G.J. McIlraith   6 Jul 1968–21 Dec 1970
J.P. Goyer   22 Dec 1970–26 Nov 1972
W. Allmand   27 Nov 1972–14 Sep 1976
F. Fox   15 Sep 1976–

Minister of Public Works
G.J. McIlraith   20 Apr 1968–5 Jul 1968

A. Laing	6 Jul 1968–27 Jan 1972
J.E. Dubé	28 Jan 1972–7 Aug 1974
C.M. Drury	8 Aug 1974–14 Sep 1976
J.J. Buchanan	15 Sep 1976–

Minister of Manpower and Immigration

J. Marchand	20 Apr 1968–5 Jul 1968
A.J. MacEachen	6 Jul 1968–23 Sep 1970
O.E. Lang	24 Sep 1970–27 Jan 1972
B.S. Mackasey	28 Jan 1972–26 Nov 1972
R.K. Andras	27 Nov 1972–14 Sep 1976
J.S.G. Cullen	15 Sep 1976–

President of the Treasury Board

E. Benson	20 Apr 1968–5 Jul 1968
C.M. Drury	6 Jul 1968–7 Aug 1974
J. Chrétien	8 Aug 1974–14 Sep 1976
R.K. Andras	15 Sep 1976–

Secretary of State for Canada

J. Marchand	20 Apr 1968–5 Jul 1968
G. Pelletier	6 Jul 1968–26 Nov 1972
J.H. Faulkner	27 Nov 1972–14 Sep 1976
J. Roberts	15 Sep 1976–

Minister of Fisheries

H. Robichaud	20 Apr 1968–5 Jul 1968
J. Davis	6 Jul 1968–31 Mar 1969

Minister of Fisheries and Forestry

J. Davis	1 Apr 1969–10 Jun 1971

Minister of Agriculture

J.J. Greene	20 Apr 1968–5 Jul 1968
H.A. Olson	6 Jul 1968–26 Nov 1972
E.F. Whelan	27 Nov 1972–

Minister of Consumer and Corporate Affairs

J.N. Turner	20 Apr 1968–5 Jul 1968
S.R. Basford	6 Jul 1968–27 Jan 1972
R.K. Andras	28 Jan 1972–26 Nov 1972
H.E. Gray	27 Nov 1972–7 Aug 1974
A. Ouellet	8 Aug 1974–16 Mar 1976
B.S. Mackasey (Acting)	17 Mar 1976–7 Apr 1976
B.S. Mackasey	8 Apr 1976–14 Sep 1976
A. Abbott	15 Sep 1976–

Minister of Veterans' Affairs

R.J. Teillet	20 Apr 1968—5 Jul 1968
J.E. Dubé	6 Jul 1968—27 Jan 1972
A. Laing	28 Jan 1972—26 Nov 1972
D.J. MacDonald	27 Nov 1972—

Minister of Defence Production

C.M. Drury	20 Apr 1968—5 Jul 1968
D.C. Jamieson	6 Jul 1968—30 Mar 1969

Postmaster General

J.-P. Côté	20 Apr 1968—5 Jul 1968
E.W. Kierans	6 Jul 1968—28 Apr 1971
J.-P. Côté (Acting)	29 Apr 1971—10 Jun 1971
J.-P. Côté	11 Jun 1971—26 Nov 1972
A. Ouellet	27 Nov. 1972—7 Aug 1974
B.S. Mackasey	8 Aug 1974—14 Sep 1976
J.-J. Blais	15 Sep 1976—

* Responsibility for Post Office delegated to J.-P. Côté, Minister Without Portfolio, 24 Sep 1970—10 Jun 1971.

Minister of Finance and Receiver General

E. Benson	20 Apr 1968—31 Mar 1969

Minister of Finance

E. Benson	1 Apr 1969—27 Jan 1972
J.N. Turner	28 Jan 1972—11 Sep 1975
C.M. Drury (Acting)	12 Sep 1975—25 Sep 1975
D.S. Macdonald	26 Sep 1975—

Minister of National Defence

L.A.J. Cadieux	20 Apr 1968—16 Sep 1970
C.M. Drury (Acting)	17 Sep 1970—23 Sep 1970
D.S. Macdonald	24 Sep 1970—27 Jan 1972
E. Benson	28 Jan 1972—31 Aug 1972
J.E. Dubé (Acting)	1 Sep 1972—6 Sep 1972
C.M. Drury (Acting)	7 Sep 1972—26 Nov 1972
J.A. Richardson	27 Nov 1972—15 Oct 1976
B.J. Danson (Acting)	16 Oct 1976—3 Nov 1976
B.J. Danson	4 Nov 1976—

Minister of Industry

C.M. Drury	20 Apr 1968—5 Jul 1968
J.-L. Pepin	6 Jul 1968—31 Mar 1969

Minister of Trade and Commerce

C.M. Drury	20 Apr 1968—5 Jul 1968

J.-L. Pepin   6 Jul 1968–31 Mar 1969

Minister of Industry, Trade and Commerce
J.-L. Pepin   1 Apr 1969–26 Nov 1972
A.W. Gillespie   27 Nov 1972–25 Sep 1975
D.C. Jamieson   26 Sep 1975–14 Sep 1976
J. Chrétien   15 Sep 1976–

Minister of Forestry and Rural Development
M. Sauvé   20 Apr 1968–5 Jul 1968
J. Marchand   6 Jul 1968–31 Mar 1969

Minister of Regional Economic Expansion
J. Marchand   1 Apr 1969–26 Nov 1972
D.C. Jamieson   27 Nov 1972–25 Sep 1975
M. Lessard   26 Sep 1975–

Minister of Energy, Mines and Resources
J.-L. Pepin   20 Apr 1968–5 Jul 1968
J.J. Greene   6 Jul 1968–27 Jan 1972
D.S. Macdonald   28 Jan 1972–25 Sep 1975
A.W. Gillespie   26 Sep 1975–

Minister of National Revenue
J. Chrétien   20 Apr 1968–5 Jul 1968
J.-P. Côté   6 Jul 1968–23 Sep 1970
H.E. Gray   24 Sep 1970–26 Nov 1972
R.D.G. Stanbury   27 Nov 1972–7 Aug 1974
S.R. Basford   8 Aug 1974–25 Sep 1975
J.S.G. Cullen   26 Sep 1975–14 Sep 1976
M. Bégin   15 Sep 1976–

Minister of Justice and Attorney General
P.E. Trudeau   20 Apr 1968–5 Jul 1968
J.N. Turner   6 Jul 1968–27 Jan 1972
O.E. Lang   28 Jan 1972–25 Sep 1975
S.R. Basford   26 Sep 1975–

Minister of Indian Affairs and Northern Development
A. Laing   20 Apr 1968–5 Jul 1968
J. Chrétien   6 Jul 1968–7 Aug 1974
J. J. Buchanan   8 Aug 1974–14 Sep 1976
W. Allmand   15 Sep 1976–

Minister of Labour
J.-L. Pepin   20 Apr 1968–5 Jul 1968
B.S. Mackasey   6 Jul 1968–27 Jan 1972

| M.P. O'Connell | 28 Jan 1972–26 Nov 1972 |
| J.C. Munro | 27 Nov 1972– |

President of the Privy Council

P.E. Trudeau (Acting)	20 Apr 1968–1 May 1968
A.J. MacEachen (Acting)	2 May 1968–5 Jul 1968
*D.S. Macdonald	6 Jul 1968–23 Sep 1970
*A.J. MacEachen	24 Sep 1970–7 Aug 1974
*M.W. Sharp	8 Aug 1974–14 Sep 1976
*A.J. MacEachen	15 Sep 1976–

*Also Government House Leaders.

Minister of National Health and Welfare

A.J. MacEachen	20 Apr 1968–5 Jul 1968
J.C. Munro	6 Jul 1968–26 Nov 1972
M. Lalonde	27 Nov 1972–

Member of the Administration and Minister Without Portfolio

P.J.J. Martin (Leader of Government in Senate)	20 Apr 1968–31 Mar 1969
J.C. Munro	20 Apr 1968–5 Jul 1968
G. Pelletier	20 Apr 1968–5 Jul 1968
J. Davis	26 Apr 1968–5 Jul 1968
C.R.M. Granger	20 Apr 1968–5 Jul 1968
B.S. Mackasey	20 Apr 1968–5 Jul 1968
D.S. Macdonald	20 Apr 1968–5 Jul 1968
R.K. Andras	6 Jul 1968–29 Jun 1971
J.A. Richardson	6 Jul 1968–4 May 1969
O.E. Lang	6 Jul 1968–23 Sep 1970
H.E. Gray	20 Oct 1969–23 Sep 1970
R.D.G. Stanbury	20 Oct 1969–11 Aug 1971
J.-P. Côté	24 Sep 1970–10 Jun 1971*
J. Marchand	26 Sep 1975–21 Jan 1976
J.-P. Guay	4 Nov 1976–

*Responsible for Post Office.

Leader of the Government in the Senate

| P.J.J. Martin | 1 Apr 1969–7 Aug 1974 |
| R. Perrault | 8 Aug 1974– |

Minister of Supply and Services and Receiver General

D.C. Jamieson	1 Apr 1969–4 May 1969
J.A. Richardson	5 May 1969–26 Nov 1972
J.P. Goyer	27 Nov 1972–

Minister of Communications

| E.W. Kierans | 1 Apr 1969–28 Apr 1971 |

J.-P. Côté (Acting)	29 Apr 1971–10 May 1971
G. Pelletier (Acting)	11 May 1971–11 Aug 1971
R.D.G. Stanbury	12 Aug 1971–26 Nov 1972
G. Pelletier	27 Nov 1972–28 Aug 1975
P. Juneau	29 Aug 1975–24 Oct 1975
Vacant	25 Oct 1975–4 Dec 1975
J. Sauvé	5 Dec 1975–

(United with office of Postmaster General 1 Apr 1969–10 Jun 1971.)

Minister of the Environment and Minister of Fisheries

J. Davis	11 Jun 1971–7 Aug 1974
J. Sauvé	8 Aug 1974–4 Dec 1975
R. LeBlanc (Acting)	5 Dec 1975–21 Jan 1976
J. Marchand	22 Jan 1976–30 Jun 1976
R. LeBlanc (Acting)	1 Jul 1976–14 Sep 1976
R. LeBlanc	15 Sep 1976–

Associate Minister of National Defence

Vacant	20 Apr 1968–

Minister of State for Urban Affairs

R.K. Andras	30 Jun 1971–27 Jan 1972
S.R. Basford	28 Jan 1972–7 Aug 1974
B.J. Danson	8 Aug 1974–3 Nov 1976
A. Ouellet	4 Nov 1976–

Minister of State for Science and Technology

A. Gillespie	12 Aug 1971–26 Nov 1972
J. Sauvé	27 Nov 1972–7 Aug 1974
C.M. Drury	8 Aug 1974–14 Sep 1976
J.H. Faulkner	15 Sep 1976–

Minister of State

M.P. O'Connell	12 Aug 1971–27 Jan 1972
P.M. Mahoney	28 Jan 1972–26 Nov 1972
S. Haidasz[1]	27 Nov 1972–7 Aug 1974
B.S. Mackasey	3 Jun 1974–7 Aug 1974
L. Marchand[2]	15 Sep 1976–
I. Campagnolo[3]	15 Sep 1976–

[1] Special responsibility for Multiculturalism.
[2] Special responsibility for Small Businesses.
[3] Special responsibility for Fitness and Amateur Sport.

Minister of State (Fisheries)

R. LeBlanc	8 Aug 1974–14 Sep 1976

Source, Pages 2-18: Material from Public Archives of Canada and Privy Council Office. Reproduced by permission of the Minister of Supply and Services Canada.

4. Ministers by Department 1945–1976

Prime Minister

W.L.M. King	1945
L.S. St. Laurent	15 Nov 1948
J.G. Diefenbaker	21 Jun 1957
L.B. Pearson	22 Apr 1963
P.E. Trudeau	20 Apr 1968

Minister of Agriculture

J.G. Gardiner	1945
D.S. Harkness (Acting)	21 Jun 1957
D.S. Harkness	7 Aug 1957
F.A.G. Hamilton	11 Oct 1960
H.W. Hays	22 Apr 1963
J.J. Greene	18 Dec 1965
H.A. Olson	6 Jul 1968
E.F. Whelan	27 Nov 1972

Minister of Citizenship and Immigration

W.E. Harris	18 Jan 1950
J.W. Pickersgill	1 Jul 1954
E.D. Fulton (Acting)	21 Jun 1954
E.L. Fairclough	12 May 1958
R.A. Bell	9 Aug 1962
G. Favreau	22 Apr 1963
R. Tremblay	3 Feb 1964
J.R. Nicholson	15 Feb 1965
J. Marchand	18 Dec 1965

(Reorganized as Department of Manpower and Immigration 1 Oct 1966.)

Minister of Communications

E.W. Kierans	1 Apr 1969
J.P. Côté (Acting)	29 Apr 1971
G. Pelletier (Acting)	11 May 1971
R.D.G. Stanbury	12 Aug 1971
G. Pelletier	27 Nov 1972
P. Juneau	29 Aug 1975
J. Sauvé	5 Dec 1975

(United with office of Postmaster General 1 Apr 1969–10 Jun 1971.)

Minister of Consumer and Corporate Affairs

J.N. Turner	21 Dec 1967
S.R. Basford	6 Jul 1968
R.K. Andras	28 Jan 1972
H.E. Gray	27 Nov 1972
A. Ouellet	8 Aug 1974

B.S. Mackasey (Acting)	17 Mar 1976
B.S. Mackasey	8 Apr 1976
A. Abbott	15 Sep 1976

Minister of Defence Production

C.D. Howe	1 Apr 1951
H.C. Green (Acting)	21 Jun 1957
R.J.M. O'Hurley	12 May 1958
C.M. Drury	22 Apr 1963
D.C. Jamieson	6 Jul 1968

(Reorganized as Department of Supply and Services 1 Apr 1969.)

Minister of Energy, Mines and Resources

J.-L. Pepin	1 Oct 1966
J.J. Greene	6 Jul 1968
D.S. Macdonald	28 Jan 1972
A.W. Gillespie	26 Sep 1975

Minister of the Environment and Minister of Fisheries

J. Davis	11 Jun 1971
J. Sauvé	8 Aug 1974
R. LeBlanc (Acting)	5 Dec 1975
J. Marchand	22 Jan 1976
R. LeBlanc (Acting)	1 Jul 1976
R. LeBlanc	15 Sep 1976

(Responsibility for fisheries administration delegated to Minister of State [Fisheries] 8 Aug 1974–15 Sep 1976.)

*Minister of Finance and Receiver General**

J.L. Ilsley	1945
D.C. Abbott	10 Dec 1946
W.E. Harris	1 Jul 1954
D.M. Fleming	21 Jun 1957
G.C. Nowlan	9 Aug 1962
W.L. Gordon	22 Apr 1963
M.W. Sharp (Acting)	11 Nov 1965
M.W. Sharp	18 Dec 1965
E. Benson	20 Apr 1968
J.N. Turner	28 Jan 1972
C.M. Drury (Acting)	11 Sep 1975
D.S. Macdonald	26 Sep 1975

*After 1 Apr 1969 Minister of Finance.

Minister of Fisheries

E. Bertrand	1945

H.F.G. Bridges	29 Aug 1945
Vacant	11 Aug 1947
E. Bertrand (Acting)	14 Aug 1947
M.F. Gregg	2 Sep 1947
J.A. MacKinnon	19 Jan 1948
R.W. Mayhew	11 Jun 1948
J. Sinclair	15 Oct 1952
J.A. MacLean	21 Jun 1957
H. Robichaud	22 Apr 1963
J. Davis	6 Jul 1968

(Reorganized as Department of Fisheries and Forestry 1 Apr 1969.)

Minister of Forestry

Vacant	1 Oct 1960
H.J. Flemming	11 Oct 1960
M. Asselin	18 Mar 1963
J.R. Nicholson	22 Apr 1963
M. Sauvé	3 Feb 1964

(Reorganized as Department of Forestry and Rural Development 1 Oct 1966.)

Minister of Forestry and Rural Development

M. Sauvé	1 Oct 1966
J. Marchand	6 Jul 1968

(Reorganized as Department of Regional Economic Expansion and Department of Fisheries and Forestry 1 Apr 1969.)

Minister of Fisheries and Forestry

J. Davis	1 Apr 1969

(Reorganized as Department of the Environment 11 Jun 1971; office of Minister of the Environment and Minister of Fisheries created.)

Minister of Indian Affairs and Northern Development

A. Laing	1 Oct 1966
J. Chrétien	6 Jul 1968
J.J. Buchanan	8 Aug 1974
W. Allmand	15 Sep 1976

Minister of Industry

C.M. Dury	25 Jul 1963
J.-L. Pepin	6 Jul 1968

(Merged with Department of Trade and Commerce to form Department of Industry, Trade and Commerce 1 Apr 1969.)

Minister of Industry, Trade and Commerce

J.-L. Pepin	1 Apr 1969
A.W. Gillespie	27 Nov 1972

D.C. Jamieson	26 Sep 1975
J. Chrétien	15 Sep 1976

Minister of Justice and Attorney General

L.S. St. Laurent	1945
J.L. Ilsley	10 Dec 1946
L.S. St. Laurent (Acting)	1 Jul 1948
L.S. St. Laurent	10 Sep 1948
S.S. Garson	15 Nov 1948
E.D. Fulton	21 Jun 1957
D.M. Fleming	9 Aug 1962
L. Chevrier	22 Apr 1963
G. Favreau	3 Feb 1964
G.J. McIlraith (Acting)	30 Jun 1965
L. Cardin	7 Jul 1965
P.E. Trudeau	4 Apr 1967
J.N. Turner	6 Jul 1968
O.E. Lang	28 Jan 1972
S.R. Basford	26 Sep 1975

Minister of Labour

H. Mitchell	1945
P.J.J. Martin (Acting)	3 Aug 1950
M.F. Gregg	7 Aug 1950
M. Starr	21 Jun 1957
A.J. MacEachen	22 Apr 1963
J.R. Nicholson	18 Dec 1965
J.-L. Pepin	20 Apr 1968
B.S. Mackasey	6 Jul 1968
M.P. O'Connell	28 Jan 1972
J.C. Munro	27 Nov 1972

Leader of the Government in the Senate

P.J.J. Martin	1 Apr 1969
R. Perrault	8 Aug 1974

Minister of Manpower and Immigration

J. Marchand	1 Oct 1966
A.J. MacEachen	6 Jul 1968
O.E. Lang	24 Sep 1970
B.S. Mackasey	28 Jan 1972
R.K. Andras	27 Nov 1972
J.S.G. Cullen	15 Sep 1976

Minister of Mines and Resources

T.A. Crerar	1945

J.A. Glen	18 Apr 1945
J.A. MacKinnon	11 Jun 1948
C.W.G. Gibson	1 Apr 1949

(Reorganized as Department of Mines and Technical Surveys and Department of Resources and Development 18 Jan 1950.)

Minister of Mines and Technical Surveys

J.J. McCann	18 Jan 1950
G. Prudham	13 Dec 1950
L. Balcer (Acting)	21 Jun 1957
P. Comtois	7 Aug 1957
Vacant	7 Oct 1961
W.G. Dinsdale (Acting)	10 Oct 1961
J. Flynn	28 Dec 1961
Vacant	13 Jul 1962
H.J. Flemming (Acting)	18 Jul 1962
P. Martineau	9 Aug 1962
W.M. Benidickson	22 Apr 1963
J.W. MacNaught	7 Jul 1965
J.-L. Pepin	18 Dec 1965

(Reorganized as Department of Energy, Mines and Resources 1 Oct 1966.)

Minister of Munitions and Supply

C.D. Howe	1945

(Office abolished 31 Dec 1946.)

Minister of Northern Affairs and National Resources

J. Lesage	16 Dec 1953
D.S. Harkness	21 Jun 1957
Vacant	19 Aug 1957
F.A.G. Hamilton	22 Aug 1957
W.G. Dinsdale	11 Oct 1960
A. Laing	22 Apr 1963

(Reorganized as Department of Indian Affairs and Northern Development and Department of Energy, Mines and Resources 1 Oct 1966.)

Minister of National Defence

A.G.L. McNaughton	1945
D.C. Abbott	21 Aug 1945
B. Claxton	12 Dec 1946
R.O. Campney	1 Jul 1954
G.R. Pearkes	21 Jun 1957
D.S. Harkness	11 Oct 1960
Vacant	4 Feb 1963
G. Churchill	12 Feb 1963

P.T. Hellyer	22 Apr 1963
L.A.J. Cadieux	19 Sep 1967
C.M. Drury (Acting)	17 Sep 1970
D.S. Macdonald	24 Sep 1970
E. Benson	28 Jan 1972
J. E. Dubé (Acting)	1 Sep 1972
C.M. Drury (Acting)	7 Sep 1972
J.A. Richardson	27 Nov 1972
B.J. Danson (Acting)	16 Oct 1976
B.J. Danson	4 Nov 1976

Associate Minister of National Defence

Vacant	11 Feb 1953
R.O. Campney	12 Feb 1953
Vacant	1 Jul 1954
P.T. Hellyer	26 Apr 1957
Vacant	21 Jun 1957
J.P.A. Sévigny	20 Aug 1959
Vacant	9 Feb 1963
L. Cardin	22 Apr 1963
L.A.J. Cadieux	15 Feb 1965
Vacant	19 Sep 1967

Minister of National Defence for Air

A.L. Macdonald (Acting)	1945
C.W.G. Gibson (Acting)	11 Jan 1945
C.W.G. Gibson	8 Mar 1945

(Office discontinued 11 Dec 1946.)

Minister of National Defence for Naval Services

A.L. Macdonald	1945
D.C. Abbott	18 Apr 1945

(Office discontinued 11 Dec 1946.)

Minister of National War Services

L.R. Laflêche	1945
J.J. McCann	18 Apr 1945

(Office discontinued 18 Jan 1948.)

Minister of National Health and Welfare

B. Claxton	1945
P.J.J. Martin	12 Dec 1946
A.J. Brooks (Acting)	21 Jun 1957
J.W. Monteith	22 Aug 1957
J.V. LaMarsh	22 Apr 1963
A.J. MacEachen	18 Dec 1965

J.C. Munro	6 Jul 1968
M. Lalonde	27 Nov 1972

Minister of National Revenue

C.W.G. Gibson	1945
J.A. MacKinnon (Acting)	8 Mar 1945
D.L. MacLaren (Acting)	19 Apr 1945
J.A. MacKinnon (Acting)	30 Jul 1945
J.J. McCann	29 Aug 1945
G.C. Nowlan	21 Jun 1957
H.J. Flemming	9 Aug 1962
J.R. Garland	22 Apr 1963
Vacant	15 Mar 1964
G.J. McIlraith (Acting)	19 Mar 1964
E. Benson	29 Jun 1964
J. Chrétien	18 Jan 1968
J.-P. Côté	6 Jul 1968
H.E. Gray	24 Sep 1970
R. Stanbury	27 Nov 1972
R.D.G. Basford	8 Aug 1974
J.S.G. Cullen	26 Sep 1975
M. Bégin	15 Sep 1976

Postmaster General

W.P. Mulock	1945
Vacant	9 Jun 1945
E. Bertrand	29 Aug 1945
Vacant	24 Aug 1949
G.E. Rinfret	25 Aug 1949
A. Côté	13 Feb 1952
Vacant	8 Aug 1955
R. Pinard (Acting)	16 Aug 1955
H. Lapointe	3 Nov 1955
W.M. Hamilton	21 Jun 1957
Vacant	13 Jul 1962
J.A. MacLean (Acting)	18 Jul 1962
E.L. Fairclough	9 Aug 1962
A. Denis	22 Apr 1963
J.R. Nicholson	3 Feb 1964
R. Tremblay	15 Feb 1965
J.-P. Côté	18 Dec 1965
E.W. Kierans	6 Jul 1968
J.-P. Côté (Acting)	29 Apr 1971*
J.-P. Côté	11 Jun 1971
A. Ouellet	27 Nov 1972

B.S. Mackasey	8 Aug 1974
J.-J. Blais	15 Sep 1976

* From 29 Apr 1971 to 10 Jun 1971 responsibility for the Post Office was held by J.-P. Côté, Minister Without Portfolio.

President of the Privy Council

W.L.M. King	1945
L.S. St. Laurent	15 Nov 1948
L. Chevrier	25 Apr 1957
Vacant	21 Jun 1957
N. Dorion	28 Dec 1961
Vacant	6 Jul 1962
J.G. Diefenbaker	21 Dec 1962
M. Lamontagne	22 Apr 1963
G.J. McIlraith	3 Feb 1964
G. Favreau	7 Jul 1965
W.L. Gordon	4 Apr 1967
P.E. Trudeau (Acting)	11 Mar 1968
A.J. MacEachen (Acting)	2 May 1968
D.S. Macdonald*	6 Jul 1968
A.J. MacEachen*	24 Sep 1970
M.W. Sharp*	8 Aug 1974
A.J. MacEachen*	14 Sep 1976

*Also Government House Leader.

President of the Treasury Board

E. Benson	1 Oct 1966
C.M. Drury	6 Jul 1968
J. Chrétien	8 Aug 1974
R.K. Andras	15 Sep 1976

Minister of Public Works

A. Fournier	1945
W.E. Harris (Acting)	12 Jun 1953
R.H. Winters	17 Sep 1953
H.C. Green	21 Jun 1957
D.J. Walker	20 Aug 1959
Vacant	12 Jul 1962
H.C. Green (Acting)	18 Jul 1962
E.D. Fulton	9 Aug 1962
J.P. Deschatelets	22 Apr 1963
Vacant	12 Feb 1965
L. Cardin	15 Feb 1965
G.J. McIlraith	7 Jul 1965

A. Laing	6 Jul 1968
J.E. Dubé	28 Jan 1972
C.M. Drury	8 Aug 1974
J.J. Buchanan	15 Sep 1976

Receiver General

J.L. Ilsley	1945
D.C. Abbott	10 Dec 1946
W.E. Harris	1 Jul 1954
D.M. Fleming	21 Jun 1957
G.C. Nowlan	9 Aug 1962
W.L. Gordon	22 Apr 1963
M.W. Sharp (Acting)	11 Nov 1965
M.W. Sharp	18 Dec 1965
E. Benson	20 Apr 1968
D.C. Jamieson	1 Apr 1969
J.A. Richardson	5 May 1969
J.P. Goyer	27 Nov 1972

(Office held by Minister of Finance before 1 Apr 1969; office held by Minister of Supply and Services after 1 Apr 1969.)

Minister of Reconstruction

C.D. Howe	1945

(Office discontinued 31 Dec 1945.)

Minister of Reconstruction and Supply

C.D. Howe	1 Jan 1946
R.H. Winters	15 Nov 1948

(Office abolished 18 Jan 1950.)

Minister of Regional Economic Expansion

J. Marchand	1 Apr 1969
D.C. Jamieson	27 Nov 1972
M. Lessard	26 Sep 1975

Registrar General

G. Favreau	1 Oct 1966
J.N. Turner	4 Apr 1967

(Reorganized as Department of Consumer and Corporate Affairs 21 Dec 1967.)

Minister of Resources and Development

R.H. Winters	18 Jan 1950
J. Lesage	17 Sep 1953

(Reorganized as Department of Northern Affairs and National Resources 16 Dec 1953.)

Secretary of State for Canada

N.A. McLarty	1945
P.J.J. Martin	18 Apr 1945
C.W.G. Gibson	12 Dec 1946
F.G. Bradley	1 Apr 1949
J.W. Pickersgill	12 Jun 1953
R. Pinard	1 Jul 1954
E.L. Fairclough	21 Jun 1957
H. Courtemanche	12 May 1958
Vacant	20 Jan 1960
L. Balcer (Acting)	21 Jan 1960
N. Dorion	11 Oct 1960
Vacant	6 Jul 1962
L. Balcer (Acting)	11 Jul 1962
G.E. Halpenny	9 Aug 1962
J.W. Pickersgill	22 Apr 1963
M. Lamontagne	3 Feb 1964
J.V. LaMarsh	18 Dec 1965
J.J. Connolly (Acting)	10 Apr 1968
J. Marchand	20 Apr 1968
G. Pelletier	6 Jul 1968
J.H. Faulkner	27 Nov 1972
J. Roberts	15 Sep 1976

Secretary of State for External Affairs

W.L.M. King	1945
L. S. St. Laurent	4 Sep 1946
L.B. Pearson	10 Sep 1948
J.G. Diefenbaker	21 Jun 1957
S.E. Smith	13 Sep 1957
Vacant	18 Mar 1959
J.G. Diefenbaker (Acting)	19 Mar 1959
H.C. Green	4 Jun 1959
P.J.J. Martin	22 Apr 1963
M.W. Sharp	20 Apr 1968
A.J. MacEachen	8 Aug 1974
D.C. Jamieson	15 Sep 1976

Solicitor General

Vacant	1945
J. Jean	18 Apr 1945
Vacant	24 Aug 1949
H. Lapointe	25 Aug 1949

S.S. Garson	7 Aug 1950
R.O. Campney	15 Oct 1952
R.W. Macdonald*	12 Jan 1954
L. Balcer	21 Jun 1957
W.J. Browne	11 Oct 1960
Vacant	10 Aug 1962
J.W. MacNaught	22 Apr 1963
L.T. Pennell	7 Jul 1965
J.N. Turner	20 Apr 1968
G.J. McIlraith	6 Jul 1968
J.P. Goyer	22 Dec 1970
W. Allmand	27 Nov 1972
F. Fox	15 Sep 1976

*Also Government Leader in the Senate.

Minister of Supply and Services

D.C. Jamieson	1 Apr 1969
J.A. Richardson	5 May 1969
J.P. Goyer	27 Nov 1972

Minister of Trade and Commerce

J.A. MacKinnon	1945
C.D. Howe	19 Jan 1948
G. Churchill	21 Jun 1957
G. Hees	11 Oct 1960
Vacant	9 Feb 1963
M.W. McCutcheon	12 Feb 1963
M.W. Sharp	22 Apr 1963
Vacant	18 Dec 1965
R.H. Winters	4 Jan 1966
J.-L. Pepin (Acting)	30 Mar 1968
C.M. Drury	20 Apr 1968
J.-L. Pepin	6 Jul 1968

(Merged with Department of Industry to form Department of Industry, Trade and Commerce 1 Apr 1969.)

Minister of Transport

J.E. Michaud	1945
L. Chevrier	18 Apr 1945
G.C. Marler	1 Jul 1954
G. Hees	21 Jun 1957
L. Balcer	11 Oct 1960
G.J. McIlraith	22 Apr 1963
J.W. Pickersgill	3 Feb 1964

P.T. Hellyer	19 Sep 1967
J.A. Richardson (Acting)	30 Apr 1969
D.C. Jamieson	5 May 1969
J. Marchand	27 Nov 1972
O.E. Lang	26 Sep 1975

Minister of Veterans' Affairs

I.A. Mackenzie	1945
M.F. Gregg	19 Jan 1948
H. Lapointe	7 Aug 1950
A.J. Brooks	21 Jun 1957
G. Churchill	11 Oct 1960
M.J.A. Lambert	12 Feb 1963
R.J. Teillet	22 Apr 1963
J.E. Dubé	6 July 1968
A. Laing	28 Jan 1972
D.S. Macdonald	27 Nov 1972

Minister of State for Fisheries

R. LeBlanc	8 Aug 1974

(Office discontinued 15 Sep 1976.)

Minister of State for Urban Affairs

R.K. Andras	30 Jun 1971
S.R. Basford	28 Jan 1972
B.J. Danson	8 Aug 1974
A. Ouellet	4 Nov 1976

Minister of State for Science and Technology

A.W. Gillespie	12 Aug 1971
J. Sauvé	27 Nov 1972
C.M. Drury	8 Aug 1974
J.H. Faulkner	15 Sep 1976

Minister of State

M.P. O'Connell	12 Aug 1971 – 27 Jan 1972
P.M. Mahoney	28 Jan 1972 – 26 Nov 1972
S. Haidasz [1]	27 Nov 1972 – 7 Aug 1974
B.S. Mackasey	3 Jun 1974 – 7 Aug 1974
L. Marchand [2]	15 Sep 1976 –
I. Campagnolo [3]	15 Sep 1976 –

[1] Special responsibility for Multiculturalism.
[2] Special responsibility for Small Businesses.
[3] Special responsibility for Fitness and Amateur Sport.

Member of the Administration and Minister Without Portfolio

J.H. King*	1945–23 Aug 1945
W.M. Robertson*	4 Sep 1945–13 Oct 1953
J.A. MacKinnon	1 Apr 1949–13 Dec 1950
W.R. Macdonald*	14 Oct 1953–11 Jan 1954
J.M. Macdonnell	21 Jun 1957–19 Aug 1959
W.J. Browne	21 Jun 1957–10 Oct 1960
J.T. Haig*	9 Oct 1957–11 May 1958
G.E. Halpenny	11 Oct 1960–8 Aug 1962
M.W. McCutcheon	9 Aug 1962–11 Feb 1963
T. Ricard	18 Mar 1963–22 Apr 1963
F.C. McGee	18 Mar 1963–22 Apr 1962
W.R. Macdonald*	22 Apr 1963–2 Feb 1964
J.W. MacNaught	22 Apr 1963–6 Jul 1965
R. Tremblay	22 Apr 1963–2 Feb 1964
J.J. Connolly*	3 Feb 1964–20 Apr 1968
Y. Dupuis	3 Feb 1964–21 Jan 1965
L.T. Pennell	7 Jul 1965–30 Sep 1966
J.-L. Pepin	7 Jul 1965–17 Dec 1965
J.N. Turner	18 Dec 1965–3 Apr 1967
W.L. Gordon	9 Jan 1967–3 Apr 1967
J. Chrétien	4 Apr 1967–17 Jan 1968
C.R.M. Granger	25 Sep 1967–20 Apr 1968
B.S. Mackasey	9 Feb 1968–20 Apr 1968
P.J.J. Martin*	20 Apr 1968–31 Mar 1969
J.C. Munro	20 Apr 1968–5 Jul 1968
G. Pelletier	20 Apr 1968–5 Jul 1968
J. Davis	26 Apr 1968–5 Jul 1968
C.R.M. Granger	20 Apr 1968–5 Jul 1968
B.S. Mackasey	20 Apr 1968–5 Jul 1968
D.S. Macdonald	20 Apr 1968–5 Jul 1968
R.K. Andras	6 Jul 1968–29 Jun 1971
J.A. Richardson	6 Jul 1968–4 May 1969
O.E. Lang	6 Jul 1968–23 Sep 1970
H.E. Gray	20 Oct 1969–23 Sep 1970
R.D.G. Stanbury	20 Oct 1969–11 Aug 1971
J.-P. Côté	24 Sep 1970–10 Jun 1971[1]
R. Perrault*	8 Aug 1974–
J. Marchand	26 Sep 1975–21 Jan 1976
J.-P. Guay	4 Nov 1976–

* Government Leader in the Senate.

[1] Responsible for the Post Office.

5. Geographical Representation in Federal Cabinets

Date	Nfld.	N.S.	N.B.	P.E.I.	P.Q.	Ont.	Man.	Sask.	Alta.	B.C.	Total	In Senate
1945	—	2	1	—	5	6	1	1	1	2	20	—
20 Aug 1945	—	1	1	—	6	7	1	1	1	1	20	1
15 Nov 1948	—	1	1	—	6	7	1	1	1	1	20	1
24 Aug 1949	1	1	1	—	6	7	1	1	—	1	21	2
17 Sep 1953	1	1	1	—	6	5	1	1	1	2	20	1
21 Jun 1957	1	1	1	1	3	7	1	2	1	3	21	—
12 May 1958	1	1	1	1	4	6	1	2	1	3	21	—
9 Aug 1962	—	1	1	1	4	7	2	2	1	2	22	1
22 Apr 1963	1	1	1	—	9	10	1	—	1	2	26	1
18 Dec 1965	1	1	1	—	8	11	1	—	—	2	26	1
20 Apr 1968	1	1	1	—	11	8	1	—	—	1	24	1
6 Jul 1968	1	1	1	—	11	8	1	1	1	3	29	1
27 Nov 1972	1	1	1	1	10	11	1	1	—	2	30	1
8 Aug 1974	1	1	1	1	11	10	1	1	—	1	29	1
4 Nov 1976	1	1	1	1	10	12	1	1	—	4	32	1

Source: *Canada Year Book 1945 –*.

6. The Cabinet Committee System (1973)

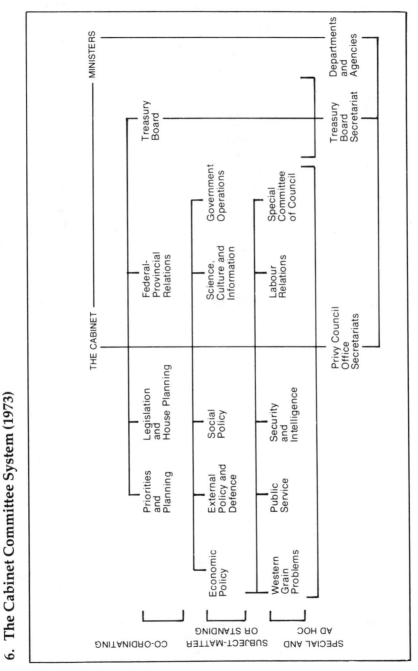

Source: *Canada Year Book 1973*, p. 71.

7. Size of Canadian Cabinets

Date	Prime Minister	Size of Cabinet
1945	King	20
29 Aug 1945	King.	20
15 Nov 1948	St. Laurent	20
24 Aug 1949	St. Laurent	21
17 Sep 1953	St. Laurent	20
21 Jan 1957	Diefenbaker	21
12 May 1958	Diefenbaker	21
9 Aug 1962	Diefenbaker	22
20 Apr 1963	Pearson	26
18 Dec 1965	Pearson	26
20 Apr 1968	Trudeau	24
6 Jul 1968	Trudeau	29
27 Nov 1972	Trudeau	30
8 Aug 1974	Trudeau	29
4 Nov 1976	Trudeau	32

Sources: *Canada Year Book 1945 — ; Guide to Canadian Ministries Since Confederation* and *Supplement, op. cit.*

8. Clerk of the Privy Council and Secretary to the Cabinet

A.D.P. Heeney	1945
N.A. Robertson	15 Mar 1949
J.W. Pickersgill	2 Jun 1952
Vacant	11 Jun 1953
R.B. Bryce	1 Jan 1954
R.G. Robertson	1 Jul 1963
P.M. Pitfield	16 Jan 1975

Secretary to the Cabinet for Federal-Provincial Relations

R.G. Robertson	16 Jan 1975

Source: *Canadian Parliamentary Guide 1945 —.*

9. Biographical Sketches of Leading Political Figures

Biographical sketches are provided for the following:

1. All persons who have held the positions of Prime Minister, Secretary of State for External Affairs, Minister of Finance or Minister of Justice since 1945.
2. All provincial premiers since 1945.
3. All national party leaders since 1945.
4. Certain other persons who, while not falling into categories 1, 2 or 3, were of such importance as to warrant inclusion.

Abbreviations:
g.e.—general election
Lib—Liberal
Cons—Conservative (before 1942)
PC—Progressive Conservative (after 1942)
CCF—Co-operative Commonwealth Federation
NDP—New Democratic Party
SC—Social Credit, Ralliement des Créditistes, Social Credit Rally
Ind—Independent

Sources: *The Canadian Directory of Parliament 1867-1967*, Ottawa: Public Archives of Canada, 1968; *Canadian Parliamentary Guide 1968-*.

Abbott, Douglas Charles
b. 1899, Lennoxville, P.Q. Educ. Bishop's College, McGill Univ., Dijon Univ. Served in Cdn. Army, R.A.F., W.W. I. Lawyer. M.P. (Lib) for St. Antoine-Westmount, 1940-54. Parliamentary Assistant to the Minister of Finance, 1944-45. Parliamentary Assistant to the Minister of National Defence, 1945. Minister of National Defence for Naval Services, 1945-46. Minister of Finance, 1946-54. Justice of the Supreme Court of Canada, 1954-73.

Anscomb, Herbert
b. 1892, England (came to Canada 1911). Chartered Accountant. Mayor of Victoria, 1929-31. M.L.A. (Cons) for Oak Bay, 1933-52. Minister of Public Works, Minister of Railways, Minister of Municipal Affairs, 1941-47. Leader of B.C. Conservative Party, 1947-52. Minister of Finance, 1946-51. d. 1972.
[Ed. Note: Although Anscomb was never Premier of B.C., the Coalition Govt. (Lib-Cons) headed by Byron Johnson was generally known as the Anscomb-Johnson Government.]

Barrett, David
b. 1930, Vancouver, B.C. Educ. Seattle University, St. Louis University. Social Worker. M.L.A. (CCF and NDP) for Coquitlam, B.C., 1960-75, Vancouver East, 1976-. Leader of B.C. NDP, 1969-. Premier and Minister of Finance, 1972-75.

Barrette, Antonio
b. 1899, Joliette, P.Q. Businessman. Unsuccessful candidate (Cons) P.Q. g.e. 1935. M.L.A. (Union Nationale) for Joliette, 1936-1960. Minister of Labour, 1944-60. Leader of Union Nationale Party, 1960-61. Premier, 1960 (8 Jan-15 Jul). d. 1968.

Basford, Stanley Ronald
b. 1932, Winnipeg, Man. Educ. Univ. of B.C. Unsuccessful candidate (Lib) in federal g.e. 1962. M.P. (Lib) for Vancouver-Burrard, 1963-68;

Vancouver Centre, 1968-. Minister of Consumer and Corporate Affairs, 1968-72. Minister of State for Urban Affairs, 1972-74. Minister of National Revenue, 1974-75. Minister of Justice and Attorney General, 1975-

Bennett, William Andrew Cecil

b. 1900, Albert County, N.B. Businessman. M.L.A. for South Okanagan, 1941-72 (as Cons 1941-51, as Ind 1951-52, as Social Credit, 1952-72). Premier, 1952-72. Minister of Finance, 1954-72. Minister of Highways, 1968 (24 Mar-25 Apr). Leader of B.C. Social Credit Party, 1952-73.

Bennett, William R.

b. 1932, Kelowna, B.C. Businessman. M.L.A. (SC) for South Okanagan, 1973 (4 Sep)-. Leader of B.C. Social Credit Party, 1973-. Premier, 1975-

Benson, Edgar John

b. 1923, Cobourg, Ont. Educ. Queen's Univ. Served in Cdn. Army, W.W. II. Chartered Accountant. M.P. (Lib) for Kingston (Ont.), 1962-68; Kingston and the Islands, 1968-72. Parliamentary Secretary to the Minister of Finance, 1963-64. Minister of National Revenue, 1964-68. President of the Treasury Board, 1966-68. Minister of Finance, 1968-72. Minister of National Defence, 1972-74. President, Canadian Transport Commission, 1974-

Bertrand, Jean-Jacques

b. 1916, Ste. Agathe-des-Monts, P.Q. Educ. Univ. of Ottawa, Univ. of Montreal. Lawyer. M.L.A. (Union Nationale) for Mississquoi, 1948-73. Parliamentary Assistant to Minister of Lands and Forests, 1954-58. Minister of Lands and Forests, 1958-60. Minister of Social Welfare and Youth, 1960 (8 Jan-15 Jul). Minister of Education, 1966-67. Minister of Justice, 1966-69. Leader of Union Nationale Party, 1968-71. Premier, 1968-70. Minister of Intergovernmental Affairs, 1968-69. d. 1973.

Blakeney, Allan E.

b. 1925, Bridgewater, N.S. Educ. Dalhousie Univ., Oxford Univ. Lawyer. M.L.A. (NDP) for Regina Centre, 1960-. Minister of Education and Minister in charge of Sask. Gov't. Insurance Office, 1960-61. Provincial Treasurer, 1961-62. Minister of Public Health, 1962-64. Leader of Sask. NDP, 1970-. Premier, 1971-. Provincial Treasurer, 1971-72. Minister of Industry and Commerce, 1971-72.

Bourassa, Robert

b. 1933, Montreal. Educ. Univ. of Montreal, Oxford Univ., Harvard Univ. Lawyer. M.L.A. (Lib) for Montreal-Mercier, 1966-76. Leader of Quebec Liberal Party, 1970-76. Premier, 1970-76.

Bracken, John

b. 1883, Ellesville, Ont. Educ. Ont. Agricultural College, Univ. of Illinois. Agricultural Scientist. Prof., Univ. of Saskatchewan, 1910-20. President,

Manitoba Agricultural College, 1920-22. M.L.A. for The Pas (Man.), 1922-43 (United Farmers of Man., 1922-28; Progressive, 1928-31; Liberal-Progressive, 1931-40; Coalition, 1940-43). Premier of Man., 1922-43. Leader of the Progressive Conservative Party of Canada, 1942-48. Leader of the Opposition, 1942-48. M.P. (PC) for Neepawa (Man.), 1945-49. Unsuccessful candidate (PC) federal g.e. 1949, Brandon (Man.), 1949. d. 1969.

Broadbent, John Edward
b. 1936, Oshawa, Ont. Educ. Univ. of Toronto, London School of Economics. Political Scientist. M.P. (NDP) for Oshawa-Whitby (Ont.), 1968-. Unsuccessful candidate for national NDP leadership, 1971. Leader of NDP in Parliament, 1974-75. National Leader of NDP, 1975-

Campbell, Alexander B.
b. 1933, Summerside, P.E.I. Educ. Dalhousie Univ. Lawyer. Leader P.E.I. Liberal Party, 1965-. M.L.A. (Lib) for 5th Prince, 1965 (9 Feb.)-. Premier, 1966-. Attorney General, 1966-69. Minister of Development, 1969-72. Minister of Agriculture and Forestry, 1972-74. Minister of Justice and Attorney General, 1974-

Campbell, Douglas L.
M.L.A. (United Farmers of Man., Liberal-Progressive) for Lakeside, 1922-69. Minister of Agriculture and Immigration, 1936-48. Premier, Minister of Dominion Provincial Relations, 1948-58. Provincial Treasurer, 1950-51. Leader of Man. Liberal Party, 1948-61.

Caouette, David-Réal
b. 1917, Amos, P.Q. Educ. Sacred Heart Commercial College, Victoriaville, P.Q. Automobile Dealer. Unsuccessful candidate in P.Q. g.e. 1944 and 1956 (SC and Lib candidate respectively). Unsuccessful candidate (SC) federal g.e. 1945, Pontiac (P.Q.). M.P. (SC) for Pontiac (P.Q.) 1946 (16 Sep)-1949. Unsuccessful candidate (SC) federal g.e. 1949, 1957, 1958, Villeneuve (P.Q.). M.P. (SC) for Villeneuve (P.Q.), 1962-68, Temiscamingue (P.Q.) 1968-76. Associate Leader, Social Credit Party of Canada, 1961-63. Leader, Ralliement des Créditistes/Social Credit Rally, 1963-71. Leader, Social Credit Party of Canada, 1971-76. d. 1976.

Cardin, Louis Joseph Lucien
b. 1919, Providence, Rhode Island, U.S.A. (came to Canada 1931). Educ. Loyola College, Univ. of Montreal. Lawyer. Served in R.C.N., W.W. II. M.P. (Lib) for Richelieu-Verchères, 1952-67. Assoc. Minister of National Defence, 1963-65. Minister of Public Works, 1965. Minister of Justice and Attorney General, 1965-67.

Chevrier, Lionel
b. 1903, Cornwall, Ont. Educ. Univ. of Ottawa, Osgoode Hall. Lawyer.

M.P. (Lib) for Stormont (Ont.), 1935-54; Montreal-Laurier, 1957-64. Parliamentary Assistant to the Minister of Munitions and Supply, 1943-45. Minister of Transport, 1945-54. President, St. Lawrence Seaway Authority, 1954-57. President of the Privy Council, 1957. Minister of Justice, 1963-64. Cdn. High Commissioner to the U.K., 1964-67. Commissioner General for State Visits, 1967. Head of Special Cdn. Mission to French Speaking Africa, 1968. Head of Special Cdn. Mission to Cdn. Consular Posts in the U.S., 1968.

Clark, Charles Joseph
b. 1939, High River, Alberta. Educ. Univ. of Alberta, Dalhousie Univ. Univ. Lecturer and Journalist. National President, PC Student Federation, 1963-65. First Vice-President, PC Association of Alberta, 1966-67. Special Assistant to the Hon. Davie Fulton, 1967. Unsuccessful candidate (PC) Alberta g.e., 1967. Executive Assistant to the Hon. Robert Stanfield, 1967. M.P. (PC) for Rocky Mountain (Alberta), 1972-. Leader of the Progressive Conservative Party of Canada, 1976-. Leader of the Opposition, 1976-

Coldwell, James William
b. 1888, Devon, England. Educ. Univ. of Exeter. Schoolteacher and Principal. Pres., Sask. Teachers' Federation, 1926-27; Cdn. Teachers' Fed. 1928-34. Alderman, Regina, 1922-25, 1926-32. Unsuccessful candidate (Farmer-Labour) Sask. g.e. 1934. Vice-Chairman, Sask. Farmers' Political Assoc., 1929-32. Pres. Independent Labour Party of Sask., 1930-32. Leader, Farmer-Labour Party of Sask., 1932-35. Unsuccessful candidate (Progressive) federal g.e. 1925. M.P. (CCF) for Rosetown-Biggar (Sask.), 1935-58. Unsuccessful candidate (CCF) federal g.e. 1958. Nat. Secretary, CCF, 1934-37. Nat. Chairman, CCF, 1938-42. Parliamentary Leader, CCF, 1940-58. Nat. President, CCF, 1942-60. d. 1974.

Connolly, Harold Joseph
b. 1901, Halifax, N.S. Educ. St. Mary's College. Journalist. M.L.A. (Lib) for Halifax North, 1936 (2 March)-1956. Minister of Trade and Industry, 1941-50. Minister of Public Health and Minister of Public Welfare, 1950-56. Acting Premier, 1954 (13 Apr-10 Sep).

Davis, William Grenville
b. 1929, Brampton, Ont. Educ. University of Toronto, Osgoode Hall. Lawyer. M.P.P. (PC) for Peel (1959-67), Peel North (1967-75), Brampton 1959-. Minister of Education, 1962-71. Minister of University Affairs, 1964-71. Leader of Ont. PC Party, 1971-. Premier, 1971-

Diefenbaker, John George
b. 1895, Newstadt, Ont. Educ. Univ. of Sask. Served in Cdn. Army W.W. I. Lawyer. Unsuccessful candidate (Cons) federal g.e.'s 1925 and 1926; Sask. g.e.'s 1929, 1935, 1938. Leader of Sask. Conservative Party, 1935-40.

M.P. (Cons) for Lake Centre (Sask.), 1940-53; Prince Albert 1953-. Leader of Progressive Conservative Party of Canada, 1956-67. Leader of the Opposition, 1956-57. Prime Minister, 1957-63. Secretary of State for External Affairs, 1957, 1959. President of Privy Council, 1962-63. Leader of the Opposition, 1963-67.

Douglas, Thomas Clement
b. 1904, Falkirk, Scotland (came to Canada 1910). Educ. Brandon College, McMaster Univ., Univ. of Chicago. Printer and Baptist Minister. Unsuccessful candidate (Farmer-Labour) Sask. g.e. 1934. M.L.A. (CCF) for Weyburn, 1944-1961. Leader of Sask. CCF, 1941-61. Premier of Sask., 1944-61. Pres. of the Exec. Council and Minister of Public Health, 1944-49. Minister of Co-operation and Co-operative Development, 1949-60. Minister in Charge of the Liquor Board, 1960-61. M.P. (CCF) for Weyburn (Sask.), 1935-44. Unsuccessful candidate (NDP) federal g.e. 1962 (Regina City). M.P. (NDP) for Burnaby-Coquitlam (B.C.), 1962 (22 Oct)-1968. Unsuccessful candidate federal g.e. 1968 (Burnaby-Seymour, B.C.). M.P. (NDP) for Nanaimo-Cowichan-The Islands (B.C.), 1969 (10 Feb)-. Leader, New Democratic Party of Canada, 1961-71.

Drew, George Alexander
b. 1894, Guelph, Ont. Educ. Univ. of Toronto, Osgoode Hall. Lawyer. Served in Cdn. Army W. W. I. Alderman, Guelph, 1922-24; Mayor, 1925. Chairman, Ontario Securities Commission, 1931-34. Leader of Ont. Conservative Party, 1938-48. M.P.P. (Cons) for Simcoe-East, 1938-48. Premier of Ontario and Minister of Education, 1943-48. M.P. (PC) for Carleton (Ont.), 1948-57. Leader of Progressive Conservative Party of Canada, 1948-56. Leader of the Opposition, 1948-56. High Commissioner to the United Kingdom, 1957-64. d. 1973.

Duplessis, Maurice L.
b. 1890, Trois-Rivières, P.Q. Educ. Laval Univ. Lawyer. Unsuccessful candidate (Cons) P.Q. g.e. 1923. M.L.A. for Trois-Rivières, 1927-59 (Cons. 1927-36, Union Nationale 1936-59). Leader of Quebec Conservative Party, 1933-36. Leader of Union Nationale Party, 1936-59. Premier and Attorney General, 1936-39; 1944-59. d. 1959.

Favreau, Guy
b. 1917, Montreal, P.Q. Educ. Univ. of Montreal. Lawyer and Univ. Lecturer. Assistant Deputy Minister of Justice, 1955-60. M.P. (Lib) for Montreal-Papineau, 1963-67. Minister of Citizenship and Immigration, 1963-64. Minister of Justice, 1964-65. President of the Privy Council, 1965-67. Registrar General, 1966-67. Justice of the Superior Court of Quebec, 1967. d. 1967.

Fleming, Donald Methuen
b. 1905, Exeter, Ont. Educ. Univ. of Toronto, Osgoode Hall. Lawyer. Member, Toronto Board of Education, 1938; Toronto City Council,

1939-44. M.P. (PC) Toronto-Eglinton, 1945-63. Minister of Finance and Receiver General, 1957-62. Minister of Justice and Attorney General, 1962-63. Candidate for leadership of PC Party, 1967.

Flemming, Hugh John
b. 1899, Peel, Carleton Co., N.B. Businessman. Unsuccessful candidate (Cons) fed. g.e. 1935. Municipal Councillor, Carleton Co., N.B., 1921-35. M.L.A. (PC) for Carleton, 1944-60. Premier, 1952-60. Minister of Public Works, 1952. Minister of Municipal Affairs, 1958-60. Leader of N.B. PC Party, 1950-60. M.P. (PC) for Victoria-Carleton, 1960 (31 Oct)-1968, for Carleton-Charlotte, 1968-72. Minister of Forestry, 1960-62. Minister of National Revenue, 1962-63.

Fortin, André
b. 1943, Granby, P.Q. Teacher. Unsuccessful candidate (SC) federal g.e. 1965. M.P. (SC) for Lotbinière (P.Q.), 1968-. Leader, Social Credit Party of Canada, 1976-

Frost, Leslie Miscampbell
b. 1895, Orillia, Ont. Educ. Univ. of Toronto, Osgoode Hall. Lawyer. M.P.P. (Cons) for Victoria, 1937-63. Provincial Treasurer and Minister of Mines, 1943-49. Leader of the PC Party of Ont., 1949-61. Premier, 1949-61. d. 1973.

Fulton, Edmund Davie
b. 1916, Kamloops, B.C. Educ. Univ. of B.C., Oxford Univ. Lawyer. Served in Cdn. Army W.W. II. M.P. (PC) for Kamloops (B.C.), 1945-63; 1965-68. Unsuccessful candidate federal g.e. 1968 (Kamloops-Cariboo). President, Young Progressive Conservatives of Canada, 1946-49. Minister of Justice, 1957-62. Acting Minister of Citizenship and Immigration, 1957-58. Minister of Public Works, 1963. Leader, Progressive Conservative Party of B.C., 1963. Unsuccessful candidate B.C. g.e. 1963. Candidate for leadership of PC Party of Canada, 1967. Justice of B.C. Supreme Court 1973-

Gardiner, James Garfield
b. 1883, Farquhar, Ont. Educ. Manitoba College, Winnipeg. Farmer and Teacher. M.L.A. (Lib) for Qu'Appelle North (Sask.), 1914-34; Melville (Sask.), 1934-35. Sask. Minister of Highways, 1922-26. Minister of Railways, 1926-27. Premier, 1926-29, 1934-35. Provincial Treasurer, 1926-27, 1934-35. M.P. (Lib) for Melville (Sask.), 1936-58. Minister of Agriculture, 1935-57. Minister of National War Services, 1940-41. d. 1962.

Garson, Stuart Sinclair
b. 1898, St. Catharine's, Ont. Educ. Univ. of Manitoba, Mantioba Law School. Lawyer. M.L.A. (Lib) for Fairford, (Man.), 1927-48. Provincial Treasurer, 1936-48. Minister of Telephones, Minister of the Power Com-

mission, 1941. Premier, Minister of Dominion-Provincial Relations, 1943-48. M.P. (Lib) for Marquette (Man.), 1948-57. Minister of Justice and Attorney General, 1948-57. Solicitor General, 1950-52.

Gordon, Walter Lockhart
b. 1906, Toronto, Ont. Educ. Royal Military College. Chartered Accountant. Chairman, Royal Commission on Administrative Classifications within the Public Service, 1946. Chairman, Royal Commission on Canada's Economic Prospects, 1955. Member, Committee on the Organization of Government in Ontario, 1958. M.P. (Lib) for Toronto Davenport, 1962-68. Minister of Finance and Receiver General, 1963-65. Minister Without Portfolio, 1967. President of the Privy Council, 1967-68.

Green, Howard Charles
b. 1895, Kaslo, B.C. Educ. Univ. of Toronto, Osgoode Hall. Lawyer. Served in Cdn. Army, W.W. I. M.P. (Cons) for Vancouver South, 1935-49; Vancouver-Quadra, 1949-62. Unsuccessful candidate (PC) federal g.e. 1963, 1965 (Vancouver-Quadra). Minister of Public Works, 1957-59. Acting Minister of Defence Production, 1957-58. Secretary of State for External Affairs, 1959-63.

Harris, Walter Edward
b. 1904, Kimberly, Ont. Lawyer and Business Executive. M.P. (Lib) for Grey-Bruce (Ont.), 1940-57. Parliamentary Assistant to the Secretary of State for External Affairs, 1947-48. Parliamentary Assistant to the Prime Minister, 1948-50. Minister of Citizenship and Immigration, 1950-54. Minister of Finance, 1954-57.

Hart, John
b. 1879, Leitrim, Ireland (came to Canada, 1898). Businessman. M.L.A. (Lib) for Victoria, 1916-24; 1933-47. Minister of Finance, 1917-24. Minister of Industries, 1922-24. Minister of Finance, 1933-47. Minister of Industry, 1933-37. Leader of B.C. Liberal Party, 1941-47. Premier, 1941-47.

Hatfield, Richard Bennett
b. 1931, Woodstock, N.B. Educ. Acadia Univ., Dalhousie Univ. Lawyer. M.L.A. (PC) for Carleton, 1961 (19 Jun)-. Leader of N.B. PC Party, 1969-. Premier, 1970-

Hellyer, Paul Theodore
b. 1923, Waterford, Ont. Educ. Curtiss-Wright Technical Institute of Aeronautics, Univ. of Toronto. Engineer and Businessman. Served in Cdn. forces, W.W. II. M.P. for Toronto-Trinity, 1958 (Dec.)-74, (1958-71 as Lib, 1971-72 as Ind, 1972-74 as PC). Unsuccessful candidate (PC) federal g.e. 1974. Parliamentary Assistant to the Minister of National

Defence, 1956-57. Associate Minister of Defence, 1957. Minister of National Defence, 1963-67. Minister of Transport, 1967-69. Resigned from Liberal caucus, May 1971. Joined PC Party, 1972. Candidate for leadership of PC Party of Canada, 1976.

Hicks, Henry Davies
b. 1915, Bridgetown, N.S. Educ. Mount Allison Univ., Dalhousie Univ., Oxford Univ. Lawyer. M.L.A. (Lib) for Annapolis and Annapolis East, 1945-60. Minister of Education, 1949-. Leader of N.S. Liberal Party, 1954-61. Premier, Provincial Treasurer, Minister of Education, 1954-56. Senator, 1972-. President, Dalhousie Univ., 1963-

Howe, Clarence Decatur
b. 1886 Waltham, Mass., U.S.A. (came to Canada 1908). Educ. Massachusetts Institute of Technology. Engineer. M.P. (Lib) for Port Arthur (Ont.), 1935-57. Minister of Railways and Canals and Minister of Marine, 1935-36. Minister of Transport, 1936-40. Minister of Munitions and Supply, 1940-45. Minister of Reconstruction, 1944-45. Minister of Reconstruction and Supply, 1945-48. Minister of Trade and Commerce, 1948-57. Minister of Defence Production, 1951-57. d. 1960.

Ilsley, James Lorimer
b. 1894, Somerset, King's County, N.S. Educ. Acadia Univ., Dalhousie Univ. Lawyer. M.P. (Lib) for Hants-King's (N.S.), 1926-35; Annapolis-King's (N.S.), 1935-49. Minister of National Revenue, 1935-40. Minister of Finance, 1940-46. Minister of Justice, 1946-48. Chief Justice, Supreme Court of Nova Scotia, 1950-67. d. 1967.

Jamieson, Donald Campbell
b. 1921, St. John's Nfld. Businessman and Broadcaster. Pres., Can. Assoc. of Broadcasters, 1961-65. M.P. (Lib) for Burin-Burgeo (Nfld.) 1966 (Sep 19)-. Minister of Defence Production, 1968-69. Minister of Transport, 1969-72. Minister of Regional Economic Expansion, 1972-75. Minister of Industry, Trade and Commerce, 1975-76. Secretary of State for External Affairs, 1976-

Johnson, Byron Ingemar
b. 1890, Victoria B.C. Businessman. M.P. (Lib) for Victoria, 1933-37. M.L.A. (Lib) for New Westminster, 1945-52. Leader of B.C. Liberal Party, 1947-52. Premier, 1947-52. Minister of Finance, 1952. d. 1964.

Johnson, Daniel
b. 1915, Danville, P.Q. Educ. Univ. of Montreal. Lawyer. M.L.A. (Union Nationale) for Bagot, 1946 (18 Dec)-1968. Parliamentary Assistant to the Premier, 1954-55. Deputy Speaker, 1956-58. Minister of Hydraulic Resources, 1958-60. Leader of Union Nationale Party, 1961-68. Premier and

Minister of Federal-Provincial Affairs, 1966-68. Minister of National Resources, 1966-67. d. 1968.

Jones, Walter John
b. 1878, Pownall, P.E.I. Educ. Acadia, Toronto, Chicago, Cornell Universities. Farmer and Agricultural Scientist. M.L.A. (Lib) for 4th Queen's, 1935-53. Leader of P.E.I. Liberal Party, 1943-53. Premier, 1943-53. Senator, 1953-54. d. 1954.

Kennedy, Thomas Laird
b. 1879, Dixie, Ont. Farmer. M.P.P. (Cons) for Peel, 1919-34; 1937-59. Minister of Agriculture, 1930-34; 1943-48. Premier, 1948-49. Minister of Agriculture, 1949-52. d. 1959.

King, William Lyon Mackenzie
b. 1874, Berlin (now Kitchener), Ont. Educ. Univ. of Toronto, Chicago and Harvard Univs. Economist. Deputy Minister of Labour and Editor of *Labour Gazette*, 1900-1908. M.P. (Lib) for Waterloo North (Ont.), 1908-11. Unsuccessful candidate (Lib), federal g.e. 1911, 1917 (Waterloo North and York North, Ont.) M.P. for Prince, (P.E.I.), 1919-21, York North, (Ont.), 1921-25. Unsuccessful candidate (Lib) federal g.e. 1925. M.P. for Prince Albert, (Sask.) 1926-45. Unsuccessful candidate (Lib) federal g.e. 1945. M.P. for Glengarry, (Ont.), 1945-49. Minister of Labour, 1909-11. Leader of the Liberal Party of Canada, 1919-48. Leader of the Opposition, 1919-21. Prime Minister, President of the Privy Council, Secretary of State for External Affairs, 1921-26 (June 28) and 1926 (Sept. 25)-1930. Leader of the Opposition, 1930-35. Prime Minister, President of the Privy Council, 1935-48. Secretary of State for External Affairs, 1935-46. d. 1950.

Lang, Otto Emil
b. 1932, Handel, Sask. Educ. Univ. of Sask., Oxford Univ. Lawyer and Univ. Administrator. M.P. (Lib) for Saskatoon-Humboldt, 1968-. Minister Without Portfolio, 1968-70. Minister of Manpower and Immigration, 1970-72. Minister of Justice and Attorney General, 1972-75. Minister of Transport, 1975-

Lesage, Jean
b. 1912, Montreal. Educ. Laval Univ. Lawyer. M.P. (Lib) for Montmagny-L'Islet, 1945-58 (13 Jun). Parliamentary Assistant to Secretary of State for External Affairs, 1951-52; to Minister of Finance, 1953. Minister of Resources and Development, 1953 (17 Sep-15 Dec). Minister of Northern Affairs and National Resources, 1953-57. Leader of Quebec Liberal Party, 1958-69. M.L.A. (Lib) for Quebec West, 1960-70. Premier, 1960-66. Minister of Finance, 1960-61. Minister of Federal-Provincial Affairs, 1961-66.

Lévesque, René
b. 1922, New Carlisle, P.Q. Educ. Laval Univ. Journalist and Broadcaster, M.L.A. for Laurier, 1960-70 (as Lib 1960-68; Ind 1968-69; Parti Québecois 1969-70), M.L.A. (Parti Québecois) for Taillon, 1976-. Minister of Public Works and Minister for Hydraulic Resources, 1960-61. Minister of Natural Resources, 1961-65. Minister of Family and Social Welfare, 1965-66. Leader of Parti Québecois, 1968-. Premier, 1976-

Lewis, David
b. 1909, Swislocz, Poland. Educ. McGill Univ., Oxford Univ. Lawyer. Unsuccessful candidate (CCF) federal g.e. 1940 (York-West, Ont.); by-election 1943 (Montreal-Cartier); federal g.e. 1945, 1949 (Hamilton-West, Ont.). M.P. (NDP) for York-South (Ont.), 1965-74. Unsuccessful candidate federal g.e. 1963, 1974 (York-South, Ont.). Nat. Secretary, CCF, 1937-50. Nat. Vice Chairman, CCF, 1950-54. Nat. Chairman, CCF, 1954-58. Nat. President, CCF, 1958-61. Leader New Democratic Party of Canada, 1971-75.

Lloyd, Woodrow S.
b. 1913, Webb, Sask. Teacher. M.L.A. (CCF) for Biggar, 1944-71. Minister of Education, 1944-60. Provincial Treasurer, 1960-61. Leader of Sask. CCF Party (Sask. section of NDP), 1961-70. Premier, 1961-64. d. 1972.

Lougheed, E. Peter
b. 1928, Calgary, Alta. Educ. Univ. of Alberta, Harvard Univ. Lawyer. M.L.A. (PC) for Calgary West, 1967-. Leader of Alta. PC Party, 1966-. Premier, 1971.

Low, Solon Earl
b. 1900, Cardston, Alta. Educ. Calgary Normal College, Univ. of Alta., Univ. of Southern Calif. Schoolteacher and Principal. M.L.A. (SC) for Warner (Alta.), 1935-40. Unsuccessful candidate Alta. g.e. 1940. M.L.A. (SC) for Vegreville, 1940 (June)-1944. M.L.A. (SC) for Warner, 1944-45. Prov. Treasurer of Alta., 1937-43. Prov. Treasurer and Minister of Education, 1943-44. Minister Without Portfolio, 1944-45. M.P. (SC) for Peace River (Alta.), 1945-58. Unsuccessful candidate federal g.e. 1958. President and National Leader Social Credit Assoc. of Canada, 1948-58. d. 1962.

Macdonald, Angus L.
b. 1890, Dunvegan, Inverness Co., N.S. Educ. St. Francis Xavier Univ., Dalhousie Univ., Harvard Univ. Lawyer. M.L.A. (Lib) for Halifax South, 1933-40; 1945-54. Leader of N.S. Liberal Party, 1933-40; 1945-54. Unsuccessful candidate (Lib) in fed. g.e. 1930. M.P. (Lib) for Kingston (Ont.), 1940 (12 Aug)-1945. Minister of National Defence for Naval Services, 1940-45. Premier 1933-40; 1945-54. Provincial Secretary, 1933-40. Provincial Treasurer, 1945-54. d. 1954.

Macdonald, Donald Stovel
b. 1932. Ottawa, Ont. Educ. Univ. of Toronto, Osgoode Hall, Harvard Law School, Cambridge Univ., Lawyer. M.P. (Lib) for Toronto-Rosedale, 1962-. Parliamentary Secretary to the Minister of Justice, 1963-65. Parliamentary Secretary to the Minister of Finance, 1965-66. Parliamentary Secretary to the Minister of External Affairs, 1966-68. Parliamentary Secretary to the Minister of Industry, 1968. Minister Without Portfolio, 1968. President of the Privy Council and Government House Leader, 1968-70. Minister of National Defence, 1970-72. Minister of Energy, Mines and Resources, 1972-75. Minister of Finance, 1975-

MacEachen, Allen Joseph
b. 1921, Inverness, N.S. Educ. St. Francis Xavier Univ., Univ. of Toronto, Univ. of Chicago, Massachusetts Institute of Technology. Economist and Univ. Prof. M.P. (Lib) Inverness-Richmond (N.S.), 1953-58, 1962-68; Cape Breton Highlands-Canso, 1968-. Unsuccessful candidate federal g.e. 1958. Special Assistant and Consultant on Economic Affairs to Hon. L.B. Pearson, 1958-62. Minister of Labour, 1963-65. Minister of National Health and Welfare, 1965-68. Minister of Manpower and Immigration, 1968-70. President of the Privy Council and Government House Leader, 1970-74; 1976-. Secretary of State for External Affairs, 1974-76.

MacMillan, A. Stirling
b. 1871, Upper South River, Antigonish Co., N.S. Businessman. Unsuccessful candidate (Lib) in N.S. g.e. 1920. M.L.A. (Lib) for Hants, 1928-45. Minister of Highways, 1928-40. Premier, 1940-45.

McNair, John Babbitt
b. 1889, Andover, N.B. Educ. Univ. of New Brunswick, Oxford Univ. Lawyer. M.L.A. (Lib) for York, 1935-52. Attorney General, 1935-40. Premier, 1940-52. Chief Justice of N.B., 1955-64. Lieutenant-Governor, 1965-67. d. 1968.

Manning, Ernest Charles
b. 1908, Carnduff, Sask. Clergyman. M.L.A. (SC) for Strathcona East, 1935-68. Provincial Secretary, Minister of Trade and Industry, 1935-43. Premier, 1943-68. Provincial Treasurer, 1944-54. Senator 1970-

Marchand, Jean
b. 1918, Champlain, P.Q. Educ. Laval Univ. Labour Organizer. Organizer, Confederation of Catholic Workers (CTCC), 1944. Technical Advisor, Montreal Region, 1945. General Secretary, CTCC 1947-61. President, CNTU, 1961-65. Member, Royal Commission on Bilingualism and Biculturalism, 1963-65. M.P. (Lib) for Quebec West, 1965-68; Langelier (P.Q.), 1968-76. Minister of Citizenship and Immigration, 1965-66. Minister of Manpower and Immigration, 1966-68. Minister of Forestry and Rural Development, 1968-69. Minister of Regional Economic Expan-

sion, 1969-72. Minister of Transport, 1972-75. Minister Without Portfolio, 1975-76. Minister of the Environment, 1976. Unsuccessful candidate (Lib) Quebec g.e. 1976. Senator, 1976-

Martin, Paul Joseph James

b. 1903, Ottawa, Ont. Educ. Univ. of Toronto, Osgoode Hall, Harvard Law School, Cambridge Univ., Geneva School of International Studies. Lawyer. Unsuccessful candidate (Lib) in Ontario g.e. 1928 (Renfrew-North). M.P. (Lib) for Essex East (Ont.), 1935-68. Senator, 1968-74. Parliamentary Assistant to the Minister of Labour, 1943-45. Secretary of State, 1945-46. Minister of National Health and Welfare, 1946-57. Secretary of State for External Affairs, 1963-68. Minister Without Portfolio and Gov't. Leader in the Senate, 1968-74. High Commissioner to the U.K., 1974-

Matheson, Alexander W.

b. 1903, Belleone, P.E.I. Educ. Prince of Wales College. M.L.A. (Lib) for 4th Kings, 1940-43; 1947-66. Unsuccessful candidate in P.E.I. g.e. 1943. Minister of Health and Welfare, 1948-53. Leader of P.E.I. Liberal Party, 1953-65. Premier, 1953-59. Attorney General, 1955-59.

Moores, Frank Duff

b. 1933, Carbonear, Nfld. Businessman. M.P. (PC) for Bonavista-Trinity-Conception, 1968-71. M.H.A. (PC) for Humber West, 1971-. Leader, Nfld. Progressive Conservative Party, 1970-. Premier, 1972-. Minister of Fisheries, 1972-(28 Jan-1 May). National President, PC Association of Canada, 1969-70.

Nowlan, George Clyde

b. 1898, Havelock, Digby County, N.S. Educ. Acadia Univ., Dalhousie Univ. Served in Cdn. forces, W.W. I. M.L.A. (Cons) for King's (N.S.), 1925-33. M.P. (PC) for Annapolis-King's (N.S.), 1948-49, 1950-53; Digby-Annapolis-King's, 1953-65. Unsuccessful candidate federal g.e. 1949. President, Progressive Conservative Association of Canada, 1950-54. Minister of National Revenue, 1957-62. Minister of Finance and Receiver General, 1962-63. d. 1965.

Pearson, Lester Bowles

b. 1897, Newtonbrook, Ont. Educ. Univ. of Toronto, Oxford Univ. Served in Cdn. Forces, W.W. I. Member of Cdn. Diplomatic Service from 1928. Assistant Under-Secretary for External Affairs, 1941-44. Envoy Extraordinary and Minister Plenipotentiary to the United States, 1944-45. Canadian Ambassador to the United States, 1945-46. Under-Secretary of State for External Affairs, 1946-48. M.P. (Lib) for Algoma East (Ont.), 1948-68. Secretary of State for External Affairs, 1948-57. Leader of the Liberal Party, 1958-68. Leader of the Opposition, 1958-63. Prime Minister, 1963-68. d. 1972.

Pickersgill, John Whitney
b. 1905, Wycombe, Ont. Educ. Univ. of Manitoba, Oxford Univ. Univ. Lecturer. Appointed to Department of External Affairs, 1937. Private Secretary to the Secretary of State for External Affairs, 1942-45. Special Assistant to the Prime Minister, 1945-52. Clerk of the Privy Council and Secretary to the Cabinet, 1952-53. M.P. (Lib) for Bonavista-Twillingate (Nfld.), 1953-68. Secretary of State, 1953-54. Minister of Citizenship and Immigration, 1954-57. Secretary of State, 1963-64. Minister of Transport, 1964-67. President, Cdn. Transport Commission 1968-72.

Regan, Gerald Augustine
b. 1929, Windsor, N.S. Educ. Dalhousie Univ. Lawyer. Unsuccessful candidate (Lib) in N.S. g.e. 1956, 1960. Unsuccessful candidate (Lib) in fed. g.e. 1962. M.P. (Lib) for Halifax, 1963-65. M.L.A. (Lib) for Halifax-Needham 1967-. Leader, N.S. Liberal Party 1965-. Premier, 1970-

Robarts, John Parmenter
b. 1917, Banff, Alta. Educ. Univ. of Western Ontario, Osgoode Hall. Lawyer. M.P.P. (PC) for London North, 1951-71. Minister Without Portfolio, 1958-59. Minister of Education, 1959-63. Premier, 1961-71.

Robichaud, Louis J.
b. 1925, St. Anthony, N.B. Educ. Sacred Heart Univ., Laval Univ. Lawyer. M.L.A. (Lib) for Kent, 1952-71. Leader of N.B. Liberal Party, 1958-71. Premier, 1960-70. Attorney General, 1960-65. Minister of Youth, 1968-70. Chairman, Cdn. Section, International Joint Commission, 1971-73. Senator, 1973-

Roblin, Dufferin
b. 1917, Winnipeg, Man. Educ. Univ. of Manitoba, Univ. of Chicago. Businessman. M.L.A. (PC) for Wolseley, 1949-67. Leader, Manitoba PC Party, 1954-67. Premier, Minister of Dominion-Provincial Relations, 1958-67. Acting Provincial Treasurer and Minister charged with administration of the Insurance Act, 1958-66. Candidate for National leadership of PC Party, September 1967. Unsuccessful candidate (PC) fed. g.e. 1968, 1974.

Sauvé J. M. Paul
b. 1907, St. Benoit, P.Q. Educ. Univ. of Montreal. Lawyer. M.L.A. (Cons) Deux Montagnes, 1930 (4 Nov)-1935; 1936-60 (Union Nationale). Speaker, 1936-40. Minister of Social Welfare and Youth, 1946-59. Leader, Union Nationale Party, 1959-60. Premier, 1959 (11 Sep)-1960 (2 Jan). d. 1960.

Schreyer, Edward Richard
b. 1935, Beauséjour, Manitoba. Educ. United College, Univ. of Manitoba. University Lecturer. M.L.A. (CCF-NDP) for Rossmere, 1958-65,

1969-. M.P. (NDP) for Springfield, 1965-68; Selkirk 1968-69. Leader Manitoba New Democratic Party, 1969-. Premier, Minister of Dominion-Provincial Relations, 1969-. Minister for the Administration of the Hydro Act, 1970-. Minister for the Administration of the Manitoba Development Authority Act, 1969-70. Minister of Industry and Commerce, 1969 (17 July-18 Dec). Minister of Finance, 1972-

Sharp, Mitchell William
b. 1911, Winnipeg, Man. Educ. Univ. of Manitoba, London School of Economics. Director of Economic Policy Division, Dept. of Finance, Ottawa, 1942-51. Associate Deputy Minister of Trade and Commerce, 1951-57. Deputy Minister of Trade and Commerce, 1957-58. Vice-President, Brazilian Traction, Light and Power Co. Ltd., 1958-62. Unsuccessful candidate (Lib) federal g.e. 1962 (Toronto-Eglinton). M.P. (Lib) for Toronto-Eglinton 1963-. Minister of Trade and Commerce, 1963-65. Minister of Finance and Receiver General, 1965-68. Secretary of State for External Affairs, 1968-74. President of the Privy Council and Government House Leader, 1974-76.

Shaw, Walter R.
b. 1887. Educ. Prince of Wales College, Univ. of Toronto. Farmer and Civil Servant. Leader of P.E.I. PC Party, 1958-70. M.L.A. (PC) for 1st Queens, 1959-70. Premier, 1959-66. Minister of Agriculture, 1959-61.

Smallwood, Joseph R.
b. 1900. Gambo, Nfld. Journalist and Labour Organizer. Member of National Convention, 1946. M.H.A. (Lib) for Humber West, 1949-72; Twillingate, 1975- (as Liberal Reform 1975-76; Liberal 1976-). Secretary of Nfld. Delegation to Ottawa, 1948. Premier and Minister of Economic Development, 1949-72.

Smith, George Isaac
b. 1909, Stewiacke, N.S. Educ. Dalhousie Univ. Lawyer. M.L.A. (PC) for Colchester, 1949-74. Minister of Finance and Economics, 1962-68. Chairman, N.S. Power Commission, 1962-70. Leader of the N.S. Progressive Conservative Party, 1967-71. Premier, 1967-70. Senator, 1975-

Smith, Sidney Earle
b. 1897, Port Hood, N.S. Educ. Dalhousie Univ., Harvard Univ. Lawyer. Dean, Dalhousie Law School, President, Univ. of Manitoba, 1934-44. President, Univ. of Toronto, 1944-57. M.P. (PC) for Hastings-Frontenac (Ont.), 1957 (Nov)-1959. Secretary of State for External Affairs, 1957-59. d. 1959.

Stanfield, Robert Lorne
b. 1914, Truro, N.S. Educ. Dalhousie Univ., Harvard Univ. Lawyer. M.L.A. (PC) Colchester (N.S.), 1949-67. Leader of the Progressive Con-

servative Party of N.S., 1948-67. Premier and Minister of Education, 1956-67. M.P. (PC) Colchester-Hants (N.S.), 1967-68; Halifax (N.S.), 1968-. Leader of the Progressive Conservative Party of Canada and Leader of the Opposition, 1967-76.

St-Laurent, Louis Stephen
b. 1882, Compton, P.Q. Educ. Laval Univ. Lawyer. M.P. (Lib) for Quebec East (P.Q.), 1942-58. Minister of Justice and Attorney General, 1941-46. Secretary of State for External Affairs, 1946-48. Minister of Justice, 1948. Leader of the Liberal Party, 1948-58. Prime Minister, 1948-57. President of the Privy Council, 1948-57. Leader of the Opposition, 1957-58. d. 1973.

Strom, Harry Edwin
b. 1914, Burdett, Alta. M.L.A. (SC) for Cypress, 1955-75. Minister of Agriculture, 1962-68. Minister of Municipal Affairs, 1968 (12 July-12 Dec). Leader of Alta. SC Party, 1968-73. Premier, 1968-71.

Thatcher, W. Ross
b. 1917, Neville, Sask. Educ. Queen's Univ. Businessman. M.P. (Lib) for Moose Jaw-Lake Centre, 1945-57. Leader of Sask. Liberal Party, 1959-71. M.L.A. (Lib) for Morse, 1960-71. Premier, 1964-71. Provincial Treasurer, 1964-67. Minister of Industry and Commerce, 1967-70. d. 1971.

Thompson, Robert Norman
b. 1914, Duluth, Minn., U.S.A. (came to Canada 1918). Educ. Garbutt's Business College, Calgary; Calgary Normal School; Palmer College of Chiropractic; Bob Jones Univ., U. B. C. Teacher, Missionary and Chiropractor. Served in RCAF, Imperial Ethiopian Air Force Academy, W.W.II. M.P. Red Deer (Alta.) 1962-72 (as SC 1962-68; PC 1968-72). Unsuccessful candidate federal g.e. 1972 (PC) Surrey-White Rock, B.C. President, Social Credit Assoc. of Canada, 1960-61. Leader, Social Credit Party of Canada, 1961-67.

Trudeau, Pierre Elliott
b. 1919, Montreal, P.Q. Educ. Univ. of Montreal, Harvard Univ., Université de Paris, London School of Economics. Lawyer, Journalist, University Lecturer. Served in Privy Council Office, 1949-51. Founder and Editor of *Cité libre*, M.P. (Lib) for Montreal-Mount Royal 1965-. Parliamentary Secretary to the Prime Minister, 1966-67. Minister of Justice and Attorney General, 1967-68. Leader of the Liberal Party of Canada, 1968-. Prime Minister, 1968-

Turner, John Napier
b. 1929, Richmond, Surrey, England. Educ. St. Patrick's College, Ottawa; Univ. of British Columbia; Univ. of Oxford; Univ. of Paris. Lawyer. M.P. (Lib) for Montreal, St. Laurent-St. Georges, 1962-68; Ottawa-Carleton,

1968-76. Parliamentary Secretary to the Minister of Northern Affairs and Natural Resources, 1963-65. Minister Without Portfolio, 1965-67. Registrar General, 1967-68. Minister of Consumer and Corporate Affairs, 1968. Minister of Justice and Attorney General, 1968-72. Minister of Finance, 1972-75.

Weir, Walter C.

b. 1929, High Bluff, Man. Funeral Director. M.L.A. (PC) for Minnedosa, 1959-71. Minister of Municipal Affairs, 1961-63. Minister of Highways and Public Works, 1962-66. Minister of Highways, 1966-67. Leader of Man. PC Party, 1967-71. Premier, Minister of Dominion-Provincial Affairs, 1967-69. Minister for the Administration of the Manitoba Development Authority Act, 1968-69.

Winters, Robert Henry

b. 1910, Lunenburg, N.S. Educ. Mount Allison Univ., Massachusetts Institute of Technology. Engineer. Served in Cdn. forces, W.W.II. M.P. (Lib) for Queen's-Lunenburg (N.S.), 1945-49; Lunenburg (N.S.), 1949-53; Queen's-Lunenburg (N.S.), 1953-57. Unsuccessful candidate (Lib) federal g.e. 1957, Queen's-Lunenburg. M.P. (Lib) for York-West (Ont.), 1965-68. Parliamentary Assistant to the Minister of National Revenue, 1947-48. Parliamentary Assistant to the Minister of Transport, 1948. Minister of Reconstruction and Supply, 1948-50. Minister of Resources and Development, 1950-53. Minister of Public Works, 1953-57. President, Rio Algom Mines Ltd., Rio Tinto Dow Ltd., Preston Mines Ltd. Chief Executive, British Newfoundland Corp. Ltd., 1958-65. Minister of Trade and Commerce, 1966-68. Candidate for Leadership of Liberal Party of Canada, 1968. d. 1969.

10. Size of the Public Service
Selected Departments and Agencies

Department	Year (31 March)						
	1945	1950	1955	1960	1965	1970	1975
Agriculture	3195	6667	7679	7703	9034	9026	10086
Defence Production	3835	–	1455	1448	3633	–	–
Supply and Services	–	–	–	–	–	9268	10135
External Affairs	680	1301	1548	1889	2454	3904	5480
Fisheries	374	883	1875	1883	2135	–	–
Forestry	–	–	–	–	1107	–	–
Fisheries & Forestry	–	–	–	–	–	4365	–
Environment & Fisheries	–	–	–	–	–	–	11303
Regional Economic Expansion	–	–	–	–	–	1485	1813

continued

Department	Year (31 March)						
	1945	1950	1955	1960	1965	1970	1975
Labour	9111	7793	9368	8487	9739	6210	1518
UIC	–	–	–	–	–	–	10251
Manpower & Immigration	–	–	–	–	–	9046	13248
Citizenship & Immigration	–	2657	3855	4363	4051	–	–
Mines and Resources	3694	–	–	–	–	–	–
Mines & Technical Surveys	–	1661	1982	2355	2969	–	–
Northern Affairs & Natural Resources	–	1570	2733	3174	3293	–	–
Energy, Mines & Resources	–	–	–	–	–	5330	4007
Indian Affairs & Northern Development	–	–	–	–	–	8779	10610
Trade and Commerce	2620	3748	3685	4089	3987	–	–
Industry	–	–	–	–	376	–	–
Industry, Trade & Commerce	–	–	–	–	–	7474	2834
Statistics Canada	–	–	–	–	–	–	5746
Transport	6797	9682	11482	12003	14009	17556	20306
Veterans' Affairs	7364	15082	13483	13326	12884	11118	7667
Public Works	5845	6954	7870	7776	8506	8384	9031
National Defence	26920	16847	53909	46120	39909	39027	37290
National Health & Welfare	1302	2801	3926	4273	4778	7614	10324
National Revenue	10706	16715	14707	15349	13401	18967	27012
Finance (incl. Bank of Canada to 1965)	12772	5874	5126	5033	5019	736	1229
Treasury Board	–	–	–	–	–	3843[1]	764
Solicitor General	–	–	–	–	–	17085	8172
RCMP	499	568	6236	7479	8877	[2]	17926
Justice	1032	1556	2286	2525	3440	488	1678
Post Office	13770	19096	21320	25144	27570	[3]	55591
Communications	–	–	–	–	–	46320	2409
Consumer & Corporate Affairs	–	–	–	–	–	1462	2496
Privy Council Office	44	87	107	165	308	626	704
Governor General	10	10	24	15	19	34	78
Parliament	646	843	873	955	1074	1454	285

[1]Including NRC.
[2]Included with Solicitor General.
[3]Included with Communications.
Sources: DBS, Statistics Canada, *Federal Government Employees; Canada Year Book 1945 –*.

Total: General Government Employees*

Year (31 March)						
1945	1950	1955	1960	1965	1970	1975
115,908	127,196	181,582	182,305	188,571	244,197	319,605

*Includes departmental corporations and administrative, regulatory and special funds.

Employees in Government Enterprises

	Year (31 March)			
	1963	1968	1975	1976
Total	129,819*	126,595	133,936	132,000

*Includes administrative, regulatory and special funds.

Source: *House of Commons Debates,* 13 July 1976, p. 15296.

11. Parliamentary Assistants/Parliamentary Secretaries

Before 1959 the office of Parliamentary Assistant had no statutory basis; the appointment and salary were provided by an annual vote in the House of Commons estimates. Appointments had no fixed term but ended either by resignation or with dissolution of the House. The Parliamentary Secretaries Act 1959 provided a statutory basis for the position, limiting the term of office to twelve months (with reappointment possible) and the total number of positions to sixteen. The Government Organization Act 1971 increased this total to equal the number of ministers with portfolios (that is, excluding Ministers of State and Ministers Without Portfolio). The following table gives the number of parliamentary assistants or secretaries holding office as of January 1 of the year in question.

Year	Number	Prime Minister
1945	4	King
1946	5	King
1947	4	King
1948	10	King
1949	10	St. Laurent
1950	10	St. Laurent
1951	9	St. Laurent
1952	13	St. Laurent
1953	11	St. Laurent
1954	12	St. Laurent

continued

Year	Number	Prime Minister
1955	11	St. Laurent
1956	11	St. Laurent
1957	13	St. Laurent
1958	14	Diefenbaker
1959	—	Diefenbaker
1960	16	Diefenbaker
196	16	Diefenbaker
*1962	15	Diefenbaker
1963	16	Diefenbaker
1964	16	Pearson
1965	15	Pearson
1966	16	Pearson
1967	16	Pearson
1968	16	Pearson
1969	16	Trudeau
1970	16	Trudeau
1971	16	Trudeau
1972	27	Trudeau
1973	16	Trudeau
1974	16	Trudeau
1975	20	Trudeau
1976	27	Trudeau
1977	26	Trudeau

*Taken at 18 Jan 1962.
Sources: *Guide to Canadian Ministries Since Confederation, op. cit.; Canada Year Book 1974 —*.

12. Organization Chart: The Government of Canada

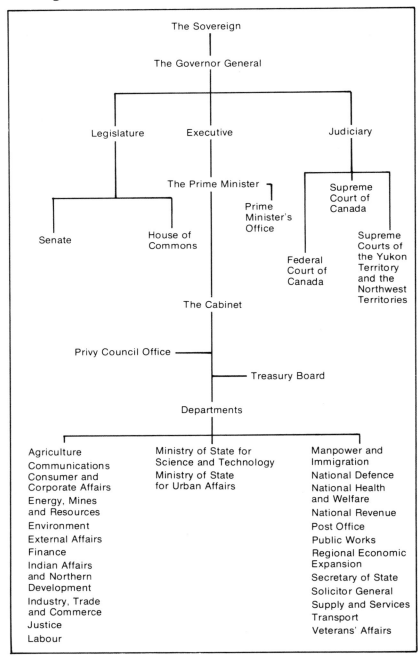

Source: *Canada Year Book 1973*, p. 93.

II
PARLIAMENT

1. Sessional Tables

Session	Opening	Prorogation	Sitting Days	Govt. Bills Introd.	Govt. Bills Passed	Priv. Members' Bills Introd.	Priv. Members' Bills Passed
19th Parliament							
6	19 Mar 45	16 Apr 45	19	4	4	0	0

Date of Dissolution: 16 Apr 45
General Election: 11 Jun 45

Session	Opening	Prorogation	Sitting Days	Govt. Bills Introd.	Govt. Bills Passed	Priv. Members' Bills Introd.	Priv. Members' Bills Passed
20th Parliament							
1	6 Sep 45	18 Dec 45	76	41	40	9	0
2	14 Mar 46	31 Aug 46	118	82	78	9	1
3	30 Jan 47	17 Jul 47	115	81	79	9	1
4	5 Dec 47	30 Jun 48	119	81	80	10	0
5	26 Jan 49	30 Apr 49	59	28	22	18	0

Date of Dissolution: 30 Apr 49
General Election: 27 Jun 49
Length of Parliament: 3yr. 8 mo. 22 d.

Session	Opening	Prorogation	Sitting Days	Govt. Bills Introd.	Govt. Bills Passed	Priv. Members' Bills Introd.	Priv. Members' Bills Passed
21st Parliament							
1	16 Sep 49	10 Dec 49	64	46	45	12	2
2	16 Feb 50	30 Jun 50	90	57	56	10	0
3	29 Aug 50	29 Jan 51	17	10	10	0	0
4	30 Jan 51	9 Oct 51	105	73	65	8	0
5	9 Oct 51	29 Dec 51	56	37	36	5	0

6	28 Feb 52	20 Nov 52	87	56	55	10	2
7	20 Nov 52	14 May 53	108	58	56	14	1

Date of Dissolution: 14 May 53
General Election: 10 Aug 53
Length of Parliament: 3 yr. 9 mo. 20 d.

22nd Parliament

1	12 Nov 53	26 Jun 54	139	67	66	15	1
2	7 Jan 55	28 Jul 55	140	61	60	15	1
3	10 Jan 56	14 Aug 56	152	51	51	23	0
4	26 Nov 56	8 Jan 57	5	2	2	0	0
5	8 Jan 57	12 Apr 57	71	45	40	16	0

Date of Dissolution: 12 Apr 57
General Election: 10 Jun 57
Length of Parliament: 3 yr. 6 mo. 5 d.

23rd Parliament

1	14 Oct 57	1 Feb 58	78	34	31	17	0

Date of Dissolution: 1 Feb 58
General Election 31 Mar 58
Length of Parliament: 5 mo. 25 d.

24th Parliament

1	12 May 58	6 Sep 58	93	47	45	17	0
2	15 Jan 59	18 Jul 59	127	56	54	28	1
3	14 Jan 60	10 Aug 60	146	51	49	50	0

continued

Session	Opening	Prorogation	Sitting Days	Govt. Bills Introd.	Govt. Bills Passed	Priv. Members' Bills Introd.	Priv. Members' Bills Passed
4	17 Nov 60	29 Sep 61	174	67	63	71	2
5	18 Jan 62	18 Apr 62	65	29	27	61	2

Date of Dissolution: 19 Apr 62
General Election: 18 Jun 62
Length of Parliament: 3 yr. 11 mo. 20 d.

25th Parliament

Session	Opening	Prorogation	Sitting Days	Govt. Bills Introd.	Govt. Bills Passed	Priv. Members' Bills Introd.	Priv. Members' Bills Passed
1	27 Sep 62	5 Feb 63	72	35	18	77	0

Date of Dissolution: 6 Feb 63
General Election: 8 Apr 63
Length of Parliament: 6 mo. 20 d.

26th Parliament

Session	Opening	Prorogation	Sitting Days	Govt. Bills Introd.	Govt. Bills Passed	Priv. Members' Bills Introd.	Priv. Members' Bills Passed
1	16 May 63	21 Dec 63	117	49	41	92	2
2	18 Feb 64	3 Apr 65	248	57	54	108	2
3	5 Apr 65	30 Jun 65	53	26	21	105	0

Date of Dissolution: 8 Sep 65
General Election: 8 Nov 65
Length of Parliament: 2 yr. 4 mo. 1 d.

27th Parliament

Session	Opening	Prorogation	Sitting Days	Govt. Bills Introd.	Govt. Bills Passed	Priv. Members' Bills Introd.	Priv. Members' Bills Passed
1	18 Jan 66	8 May 67	250	106	98	206	0
2	8 May 67	23 Apr 68	155	45	37	178	3

Date of Dissolution: 23 Apr 68
General Election: 25 Jun 68
Length of Parliament: 2 yr. 4 mo. 15 d.

28th Parliament

1	12 Sep 68	22 Oct 69	199	71	57	160	0
2	23 Oct 69	7 Oct 70	155	69	54	211	9
3	8 Oct 70	16 Feb 72	244	74	60	216	6
4	17 Feb 72	1 Sep 72	91	37	18	194	6

Date of Dissolution: 1 Sep 72
General Election: 30 Oct 72
Length of Parliament: 4 yr. 1 mo. 8 d.

29th Parliament

1	4 Jan 73	26 Feb 74	206	57	48	198	6
2	27 Feb 74	8 May 74	50	38	14	184	2

Date of Dissolution: 9 May 74
General Election: 8 Jul 74
Length of Parliament: 1 yr. 5 mo. 20 d.

30th Parliament

1	30 Sep 74	12 Oct 76	343	119	102	245	7
2	12 Oct 76						

Sources: *Journals of the House of Commons 1945 –; Canada Year Book 1945 –*.

2. House of Commons: Speakers and Deputy Speakers

Speaker	Deputy Speaker	Parlia-ment	Session
James Allison Glen	Joseph Arthur Bradette	19	6
Gaspard Fauteux	William Ross Macdonald	20	1−5
William Ross Macdonald	Joseph Alfred Dion	21	1−5
William Ross Macdonald	J.A. Dion to 8 April 52		
	Louis René Beaudoin from 8 April 52	21	6
William Ross Macdonald	Louis René Beaudoin	21	7
Louis René Beaudoin	William Alfred Robinson	22	1−5
Roland Michener	Henri Courtemanche	23	1
Roland Michener	Pierre Sévigny	24	1−2
Roland Michener	Jacques Flynn	24	3−4
Roland Michener	Paul Martineau	24	5
Marcel Lambert	Gordon Chown	25	1
Alan A. Macnaughton	Lucien Lamoureux	26	1−3
Lucien Lamoureux	Herman M. Batten	27	1−2
Lucien Lamoureux	James Hugh Faulkner to 5 October 1970 Russell Honey from 5 October 1970	28	1−2
Lucien Lamoureux	Russell Honey	28	3−4
Lucien Lamoureux	Robert McCleave	29	1−2
James Jerome	Gérald Laniel	30	1−2

Source: *Debates of the House of Commons 1945−.*

3. House of Commons: Standing and Joint Committees

Committee	Size
19th Parliament	
6th Session: 19 Mar 1945−16 Apr 1945	
Privileges and Elections	29
Railways, Canals and Telegraph Lines	61
Miscellaneous Private Bills	50
Banking and Commerce	50
Public Accounts	50
Agriculture and Colonization	61
Standing Orders	20
Marine and Fisheries	35
Mines, Forests and Waters	35

continued

Committee	Size
Industrial and International Relations	35
Debates	12
Printing (Joint)	54
Library of Parliament (Joint)	45
Restaurant of Parliament (Joint)	22

20th Parliament
1st Session: 6 Sep 1945 –18 Dec 1945

Privileges and Elections	29
Railways, Canals and Telegraph Lines	60
Miscellaneous Private Bills	50
Banking and Commerce	50
Public Accounts	50
Agriculture and Colonization	60
Standing Orders	20
Marine and Fisheries	35
Mines, Forests and Waters	35
Industrial Relations	35
Debates	12
External Affairs	35
Printing (Joint)	54
Library of Parliament (Joint)	44

2nd Session: 14 Mar 1946 –31 Aug 1946
Same as 1st Session with the deletion of Library of Parliament
Committee (Joint).

3rd Session: 30 Jan 1947 –17 Jul 1947
Same as 2nd Session with further deletion of Printing Committee
(Joint).

4th Session: 5 Dec 1947 –30 Jan 1948
Same as 2nd Session.

5th Session: 26 Jan 1949 –30 Apr 1949
Same as 1st Session with addition of Restaurant of Parliament
Committee (Joint).   24

21st Parliament
1st Session: 15 Sep 1949 –10 Dec 1949

Privileges and Elections	20
Railways, Canals and Telegraph Lines	60
Miscellaneous Private Bills	50

continued

Committee	Size
Banking and Commerce	50
Public Accounts	50
Agriculture and Colonization	60
Standing Orders	20
Marine and Fisheries	35
Mines, Forests and Waters	35
Industrial Relations	35
Debates	12
External Affairs	35
Printing (Joint)	54
Library (Joint)	44
Restaurant of Parliament (Joint)	24

2nd Session: 16 Feb 1950 – 30 Jun 1950
Same as 1st Session.

3rd Session: 29 Aug 1950 – 29 Jan 1951
Same as 1st Session.

4th Session: 30 Jan 1951 – 9 Oct 1951
Same as 1st session.

5th Session: 9 Oct 1951 – 29 Dec 1951
Same as 1st Session.

6th Session: 28 Feb 1952 – 20 Mar 1952
Same as 1st Session.

7th Session: 20 Nov 1952 – 14 May 1953
Same as 1st Session.

22nd Parliament
1st session: 12 Nov 1953 – 26 Jun 1954

Privileges and Elections	20
Railways, Canals and Telegraph Lines	60
Miscellaneous Private Bills	50
Banking and Commerce	50
Public Accounts	50
Agriculture and Colonization	60
Standing Orders	20
Marine and Fisheries	35
Mines, Forests and Waters	35
Industrial Relations	35
Debates	12

continued

Committee	Size
External Affairs	35
Printing (Joint)	54
Library (Joint)	44
Restaurant of Parliament (Joint)	24

2nd Session: 7 Jan 1955 – 28 Jul 1955
Same as 1st Session.

3rd Session: 10 Jan 1956 – 14 Aug 1956
Same as 1st Session with deletion of Restaurant of Parliament
Committee (Joint).

4th Session: 26 Nov 1956 – 8 Jan 1957
Same as 3rd Session.

5th Session: 8 Jan 1957 – 12 Apr 1957
Same as 1st Session.

23rd Parliament
1st Session: 14 Oct 1957 – 1 Feb 1958

Privileges and Elections	20
Railways, Canals and Telegraph Lines	60
Miscellaneous Private Bills	50
Banking and Commerce	50
Public Accounts	50
Agriculture and Colonization	60
Standing Orders	20
Marine and Fisheries	35
Mines, Forests and Waters	35
Industrial Relations	35
Debates	12
External Affairs	35
Printing (Joint)	54
Library (Joint)	44
Restaurant of Parliament (Joint)	24

24th Parliament
1st Session: 12 May 1958 – 6 Sep 1958

Privileges and Elections	29
Railways, Canals and Telegraph Lines	60
Miscellaneous Private Bills	50
Banking and Commerce	50
Public Accounts	50

continued

Committee	Size
Agriculture and Colonization	60
Standing Orders	20
Marine and Fisheries	35
Mines, Forest and Waters	35
Industrial Relations	35
Debates	12
External Affairs	35
Estimates	60
Veterans' Affairs	40
Printing (Joint)	23
Library of Parliament (Joint)	21
Restaurant (Joint)	26

2nd Session: 15 Jan 1959 — 18 Jul 1959
Same as 1st Session.

3rd Session: 14 Jan 1960 — 10 Aug 1960
Same as 1st Session.

4th Session: 17 Nov 1960 — 29 Sep 1961
Same as 1st Session.

5th Session: 18 Jan 1962 — 18 Apr 1962
Same as 1st Session.

25th Parliament
1st Session: 27 Sep 1962 — 5 Feb 1963

Privileges and Elections	29
Railways, Canals and Telegraph Lines	60
Miscellaneous Private Bills	50
Banking and Commerce	50
Public Accounts	50
Agriculture and Colonization	60
Standing Orders	20
Marine and Fisheries	35
Mines, Forests and Waters	35
Industrial Relations	35
Debates	12
External Affairs	35
Estimates	60
Veterans' Affairs	40
Printing (Joint)	23
Library of Parliament (Joint)	21
Restaurant (Joint)	26

continued

Committee	Size
26th Parliament	
1st Session: 16 May 1963 – 21 Dec 1963	
Privileges and Elections	29
Railways, Canals and Telegraph Lines	60
Miscellaneous Private Bills	50
Banking and Commerce	50
Public Accounts	50
Agriculture and Colonization	60
Standing Orders	20
Marine and Fisheries	35
Mines, Forests and Waters	35
Industrial Relations	35
Debates	12
External Affairs	35
Estimates	60
Veterans' Affairs	40
Printing (Joint)	23
Library of Parliament (Joint)	21

2nd Session: 18 Feb 1964 – 3 Apr 1965

Same as 1st Session with addition of Restaurant of Parliament Committee (Joint).

3rd Session: 5 Apr 1965 – 30 Jun 1965	
Broadcasting, Films and Assistance to the Arts	24
Crown Corporations	24
Finance, Trade and Economic Affairs	24
Fisheries	24
Health and Welfare	24
Housing, Urban Development and Public Works	24
Indian Affairs, Human Rights and Citizenship and Immigration	24
Industry, Research and Energy Development	24
Justice and Legal Affairs	24
Labour and Employment	24
Miscellaneous Estimates	24
Miscellaneous Private Bills	24
National Defence	24
Northern Affairs and National Resources	24
Privileges and Elections	24
Public Accounts	24
Standing Orders	24

continued

Committee	Size
Transport and Communications	24
Veterans' Affairs	24
External Affairs	24
Agriculture, Forestry and Rural Development	45

27th Parliament
1st Session: 18 Jan 1966 – 8 May 1967

Broadcasting, Films and Assistance to the Arts	24
Crown Corporations	24
Finance, Trade and Economic Affairs	24
Fisheries	24
Health and Welfare	24
Housing, Urban Development and Public Works	24
Indian Affairs, Human Rights and Citizenship and Immigration	24
Industry, Research and Energy Development	24
Justice and Legal Affairs	24
Labour and Employment	24
Miscellaneous Estimates	24
Miscellaneous Private Bills	24
National Defence	24
Northern Affairs and National Resources	24
Privileges and Elections	24
Public Accounts	24
Standing Orders	24
Transport and Communications	24
Veterans' Affairs	24
External Affairs	24
Agriculture, Forestry and Rural Development	45
Library of Parliament (Joint)	21
Printing (Joint)	23

2nd Session: 8 May 1967 – 23 Apr 1968

Same as 1st Session with addition of Restaurant of Parliament Committee (Joint).	26

28th Parliament
1st Session: 12 Sep 1968 – 22 Oct 1969

Agriculture	30
Broadcasting, Film and Assistance to the Arts	20
External Affairs and National Defence	30
Finance, Trade and Economic Affairs	20

continued

Committee	Size
Fisheries and Forestry	20
Health, Welfare and Social Affairs	20
Indian Affairs and Northern Development	20
Justice and Legal Affairs	20
Labour, Manpower and Immigration	20
Miscellaneous Estimates	20
Miscellaneous Private Bills and Standing Orders	12
National Resources and Public Works	20
Printing (Joint)	23
Privileges and Elections	20
Public Accounts	20
Regional Development	20
Transport and Communications	20
Veterans' Affairs	20
Library of Parliament (Joint)	22
Restaurant of Parliament (Joint)	20
Printing (Joint)	23

2nd Session: 23 Oct 1969 – 7 Oct 1970
Same as 1st Session.

3rd Session: 8 Oct 1970 – 16 Feb 1972
Same as 1st Session.

4th Session: 17 Feb 1972 – 1 Sep 1972
Same as 1st Session.

29th Parliament
1st Session: 4 Jan 1973 – 26 Feb 1974

Agriculture	30
Broadcasting, Films and Assistance to the Arts	20
External Affairs and National Defence	30
Finance, Trade and Economic Affairs	20
Fisheries and Forestry	20
Health, Welfare and Social Affairs	20
Indian Affairs and Northern Development	20
Justice and Legal Affairs	20
Labour, Manpower and Immigration	20
Miscellaneous Private Bills and Standing Orders	12
National Resources and Public Works	20
Privileges and Elections	20
Procedure and Organization	16
Public Accounts	20

continued

Committee	Size
Region Development	20
Transport and Communications	20
Veterans' Affairs	20
Library of Parliament (Joint)	22
Printing (Joint)	23
Regulations and Other Statutory Instruments (Joint)	12
Restaurant of Parliament (Joint)	20

2nd Session: 27 Feb 1974 — 8 May 1974
Same as 1st Session.

30th Parliament
1st Session: 30 Sep 1974 — 12 Oct 1976

Agriculture	30
Broadcasting, Films and Assistance to the Arts	20
External Affairs and National Defence	30
Finance, Trade and Economic Affairs	20
Fisheries and Forestry	20
Health, Welfare and Social Affairs	20
Indian Affairs and Northern Development	20
Justice and Legal Affairs	20
Labour, Manpower and Immigration	20
Miscellaneous Private Bills and Standing Orders	12
National Resources and Public Works	20
Privileges and Elections	20
Procedures and Organization	16
Public Accounts	20
Regional Development	20
Transport and Communications	20
Veterans' Affairs	20
Library of Parliament (Joint)	22
Printing (Joint)	23
Regulations and Other Statutory Instruments (Joint)	12
Restaurant of Parliament (Joint)	20

2nd Session: 12 Oct 1976 —
Same as 1st Session.

Source: *Journals of the House of Commons 1945 —*.

4. House of Commons: Members Elected as Independents

General Election	No. of Members Elected	
1945	5	(BC−1, PQ−4)
1949	5	(BC−1, PQ−4)
1953	3	(PQ−3)
1957	2	(PQ−2)
1958	−	
1962	−	
1963	−	
1965	2	(PQ−2)
1968	1	(Ont−1 [Speaker])
1972	2	(PQ−1; Ont−1 [Speaker])
1974	1	(NB−1)

Source: *Canada Year Book 1945 −*.

5. Clerk of the House of Commons

A. Beauchesne	1945
L.J. Raymond	16 Aug 1949
A. Fraser	6 Aug 1967

Source: *Canadian Parliamentary Guide 1945 −*.

6. Women in the House of Commons

	Years	Constituency
Dorise Nielsen (United Reform Party)	1940−1945	North Battleford, Sask.
Cora Casselman (Lib)	1941−1945	Edmonton East, Alta.
Gladys Strum (CCF)	1945−1949	Qu'Appelle, Sask.
Ellen Fairclough (PC)	1950−1963	Hamilton-West, Ont.
Margaret Aitken (PC)	1953−1962	York-Humber, Ont.
Sybil Bennett (PC)	1953−1956	Halton, Ont.
Ann Shipley (Lib)	1953−1957	Temiskaming, Ont.
Jean Casselman Wadds (PC)	1958−1968	Grenville-Dundas, Ont.
Judy LaMarsh (Lib)	1960−1968	Niagara Falls, Ont.
Margaret Macdonald (PC)	1961−1963	Kings, P.E.I.
Isabel Hardie (Lib)	1962−1963	Northwest Territories
Pauline Jewett (Lib)	1963−1965	Northumberland, Ont.
Margaret Konantz (Lib)	1963−1965	Winnipeg South, Man.
Eloise Jones (PC)	1964−1965	Saskatoon, Sask.

continued

	Years	Constituency
Margaret Rideout (Lib)	1964–1968	Westmorland, N.B.
Grace MacInnis (NDP)	1965–1974	Vancouver-Kingsway, B.C.
Flora Macdonald (PC)	1972–	Kingston and the Islands, Ont.
Monique Bégin (Lib)	1972–	Montreal-St. Michel, P.Q.
Albanie Morin (Lib)	1972–1976	Louis Hébert, P.Q.
Jeanne Sauvé (Lib)	1972–	Montreal-Abuntsic, P.Q.
Coline Campbell (Lib)	1974–	South Western Nova, N.S.
Ursula Appolloni (Lib)	1974–	York-South, Ont.
Aideen Nicholson (Lib)	1974–	Toronto-Trinity, Ont.
Simma Holt (Lib)	1974–	Vancouver-Kingsway, B.C.
Iona Compagnolo (Lib)	1974–	Skeena, B.C.
Jean Pigott (PC)	1976–	Ottawa-Carleton, Ont.

Source: *Canada Year Book 1945 –* .

7. The Senate: Speakers

Speaker	Parliament	Session(s)
T. Vien	19	5–6
J.H. King	20	1–5
E. Beauregard	21	1–6
W.M. Robertson	22	1–5
M.R. Drouin	23	1
M.R. Drouin	24	1–5
G.S. White	25	1
M. Bourget	26	1–3
S.J. Smith	27	1–2
J.P. Deschatelets	28	1–4
M.M. Fergusson	29	1–2
R. Lapointe	30	1

Source: *Debates of the Senate 1945 –* .

8. Leader of the Government in the Senate

J.H. King	1945
Vacant	24 Aug 1945
W.M. Robertson	29 Aug 1945
W.R. Macdonald	14 Oct 1953
Vacant	21 Jun 1957
J.T. Haig	9 Oct 1957

W.M. Asletine	12 May 1958
(Not a member of the government)	
A.J. Brooks	27 Sep 1962
(Not a member of the government)	
W.R. Macdonald	22 Apr 1963
J.J. Connolly	3 Feb 1964
P.J. Martin	20 Apr 1968
R. Perrault	8 Aug 1974

Source: *Journals of the Senate 1945 – .*

9. The Senate: Standing and Joint Committees

19th Parliament
6th Session: 19 Mar 1945 – 16 Apr 1945

Standing Orders
Banking and Commerce
Railways, Telegraphs and Harbours
Miscellaneous Private Bills
Internal Economy and Contingent Accounts
External Relations
Finance
Tourist Traffic
Debates and Reporting
Divorce
Agriculture and Forestry
Immigration and Labour
Commerce and Trade Relations of Canada
Public Health and Inspection of Foods
Civil Service Administration
Public Buildings and Grounds
Library (Joint)
Printing (Joint)
Restaurant (Joint)

20th Parliament
1st Session: 6 Sep 1945 – 18 Dec 1945

Standing Orders
Banking and Commerce
Railways, Telegraphs and Harbours
Miscellaneous Private Bills
Internal Economy and Contingent Accounts
External Relations

Finance
Tourist Traffic
Debates and Reporting
Divorce
Agriculture and Forestry
Immigration and Labour
Commerce and Trade Relations of Canada
Public Health and Inspection of Foods
Civil Service Administration
Public Buildings and Grounds
Library (Joint)
Printing (Joint)
Restaurant (Joint)

2nd Session: 14 Mar 1946 – 31 Aug 1946
Standing Orders
Banking and Commerce
Transport and Communications
Miscellaneous Private Bills
Internal Economy and Contingent Accounts
External Relations
Finance
Tourist Traffic
Debates and Reporting
Divorce
Natural Resources
Immigration and Labour
Canadian Trade Relations
Public Health and Welfare
Civil Service Administration
Public Buildings and Grounds
Library (Joint)
Printing (Joint)
Restaurant (Joint)

3rd Session: 30 Jan 1947 – 17 Jul 1947
Same as 2nd Session.

4th Session: 5 Dec 1947 – 30 Jan 1948
Same as 2nd Session.

5th Session: 26 Jan 1949 – 30 Apr 1949
Same as 2nd Session.

21st Parliament
1st Session: 15 Sep 1949 – 10 Dec 1949
Standing Orders
Banking and Commerce
Transport and Communications
Miscellaneous Private Bills
Internal Economy and Contingent Accounts
External Relations
Finance
Tourist Traffic
Debates and Reporting
Divorce
Natural Resources
Immigration and Labour
Canadian Trade Relations
Public Health and Welfare
Civil Service Administration
Public Buildings and Grounds
Library (Joint)
Printing (Joint)
Restaurant (Joint)

2nd Session: 16 Feb 1950 – 30 Jun 1950
Same as 1st Session.

3rd Session: 29 Aug 1950 – 29 Jan 1951
Same as 1st Session.

4th Session: 30 Jan 1951 – 9 Oct 1951
Same as 1st Session.

5th Session: 9 Oct 1951 – 29 Dec 1951
Same as 4th Session with deletion of Committee on Divorce.

6th Session: 28 Feb 1952 – 20 Mar 1952
Same as 4th Session.

7th Session: 20 Nov 1952 – 14 May 1953
Same as 4th Session.

22nd Parliament
1st Session: 12 Nov 1953 – 26 Jun 1954
Standing Orders
Banking and Commerce

Transport and Communications
Miscellaneous Private Bills
Internal Economy and Contingent Accounts
External Relations
Finance
Tourist Traffic
Debates and Reporting
Divorce
Natural Resources
Immigration and Labour
Canadian Trade Relations
Public Health and Welfare
Civil Service Administration
Public Buildings and Grounds
Library (Joint)
Printing (Joint)
Restaurant (Joint)

2nd Session: 7 Jan 1955 – 28 Jul 1955
Same as 1st Session with addition of Narcotic Drugs in Canada.

3rd Session: 10 Jan 1956 – 14 Aug 1956
Same as 1st Session.

4th Session: 26 Nov 1956 – 8 Jan 1957
Same as 1st Session.

5th Session: 8 Jan 1957 – 12 Apr 1957
Same as 1st Session.

23rd Parliament
1st Session: 14 Oct 1957 – 1 Feb 1958

Standing Orders
Banking and Commerce
Transport and Communications
Miscellaneous Private Bills
Internal Economy and Contingent Accounts
External Relations
Finance
Tourist Traffic
Debates and Reporting
Divorce
Natural Resources
Immigration and Labour
Canada Trade Relations

Public Health and Welfare
Civil Service Administration
Public Buildings and Grounds
Library (Joint)
Printing (Joint)
Restaurant (Joint)

24th Parliament
1st Session: 12 May 1958 — 6 Sep 1958

Standing Orders
Banking and Commerce
Transport and Communications
Miscellaneous Private Bills
Internal Economy and Contingent Accounts
External Relations
Finance
Tourist Traffic
Debates and Reporting
Divorce
Natural Resources
Immigration and Labour
Canada Trade Relations
Public Health and Welfare
Civil Service Administration
Public Buildings and Grounds
Library (Joint)
Printing (Joint)
Restaurant (Joint)

2nd Session: 15 Jan 1959 — 18 Jul 1959
Same as 1st Session with addition of Joint Committee on Indian Affairs.

3rd Session: 14 Jan 1960 — 10 Aug 1960
Same as 2nd Session with addition of Manpower Requirements and Utilization in Canada.

4th Session: 17 Nov 1960 — 29 Sep 1961
Same as 3rd Session.

5th Session: 18 Jan 1962 — 18 Apr 1962
Same as 1st Session.

25th Parliament
1st Session: 27 Sep 1962 — 5 Feb 1963
Standing Orders

Banking and Commerce
Transport and Communications
Miscellaneous Private Bills
Internal Economy and Contingent Accounts
External Relations
Finance
Tourist Traffic
Debates and Reporting
Divorce
Natural Resources
Immigration and Labour
Canada Trade Relations
Public Health and Welfare
Civil Service Administration
Public Buildings and Grounds
Library (Joint)
Printing (Joint)
Restaurant (Joint)

26th Parliament
1st Session: 16 May 1963–21 Dec 1963

Standing Orders
Banking and Commerce
Transport and Communications
Miscellaneous Private Bills
Internal Economy and Contingent Accounts
External Relations
Finance
Tourist Traffic
Debates and Reporting
Divorce
Natural Resources
Immigration and Labour
Canada Trade Relations
Public Health and Welfare
Civil Service Administration
Public Buildings and Grounds
Land Use in Canada
Library (Joint)
Printing (Joint)
Restaurant (Joint)

2nd Session: 18 Feb 1964–3 Apr 1965
Same as 1st Session.

3rd Session: 5 Apr 1965 – 30 Jun 1965
Same as 1st Session.

27th Parliament
1st Session: 18 Jan 1966 – 8 May 1967

Standing Orders
Banking and Commerce
Transport and Communications
Miscellaneous Private Bills
Internal Economy and Contingent Accounts
External Relations
Finance
Tourist Traffic
Debates and Reporting
Divorce
Natural Resources
Immigration and Labour
Canada Trade Relations
Public Health and Welfare
Civil Service Administration
Public Buildings and Grounds
Land Use in Canada
Library (Joint)
Printing (Joint)
Restaurant (Joint)

2nd Session: 8 May 1967 – 23 Apr 1968
Same as 1st Session.

28th Parliament
1st Session: 12 Sep 1968 – 22 Oct 1969

Standing Rules and Orders
Internal Economy and Contingent Accounts
Foreign Affairs
National Finance
Transport and Communications
Legal and Constitutional Affairs
Banking, Trade and Commerce
Health, Welfare and Science
Divorce
Library (Joint)
Printing (Joint)
Restaurant (Joint)

2nd Session: 23 Oct 1969 – 7 Oct 1970
Same as 1st Session.

3rd Session: 8 Oct 1970 – 16 Feb 1972
Same as 1st Session with deletion of Divorce; and Internal Economy and Contingent Accounts; and addition of Internal Economy, Budgets and Administration.

4th Session: 17 Feb 1972 – 1 Sep 1972
Same as 3rd Session with addition of Agriculture; and Regulations and Other Statutory Instruments (Joint).

29th Parliament
1st Session: 4 Jan 1973 – 26 Feb 1974

Standing Rules and Orders
Foreign Affairs
National Finance
Transport and Communications
Legal and Constitutional Affairs
Banking, Trade and Commerce
Health, Welfare and Science
Internal Economy, Budgets and Administration
Agriculture
Regulations and Other Statutory Instruments (Joint)
Library (Joint)
Printing (Joint)
Restaurant (Joint)

2nd Session: 27 Feb 1974 – 8 May 1974
Same as 1st Session.

30th Parliament
1st Session: 30 Sep 1974 – 12 Oct 1976

Standing Rules and Orders
Foreign Affairs
National Finance
Transport and Communications
Legal and Constitutional Affairs
Banking, Trade and Commerce
Health, Welfare and Science
Internal Economy, Budgets and Administration
Agriculture

Regulations and Other Statutory Instruments (Joint)
Library (Joint)
Printing (Joint)
Restaurant (Joint)

2nd Session: 12 Oct 1976 —
Same as 1st Session.
Source: *Journals of the Senate 1945 —.*

10. Clerk of the Senate and Clerk of the Parliaments

L.C. Moyer	1945
J.F. MacNeill	22 Oct 1955
R. Fortier	1 Feb 1968

Source: *Canadian Parliamentary Guide 1945 —.*

11. Officers of Parliament

Auditor General

R.W. Sellar	1945
A.M. Henderson	1 Mar 1960
G.R. Long (Acting)	24 Mar 1973
J.J. Macdonell	1 Jul 1973

Chief Electoral Officer

J. Castonguay	1945
N.J. Castonguay	4 Oct 1949
J.M. Hamel	6 Jun 1966

Representation Commissioner

N.J. Castonguay	23 Dec 1963

Source: *Canadian Parliamentary Guide 1945 —.*

12. Pay and Allowances of Members of Parliament

As of 1 Jan 1977 pay and allowances of all Members of Parliament will be escalated annually by the increase in the industrial composite wage index, subject to a 7% maximum.

Governor General

Date Effective	Sessional Indemnity
1945	$48,666.63

Members of the House of Commons

Date Effective	Sessional Indemnity	Non-Taxable Expense Allowance
1945	$4,000[1]	$2,000 p.a.
1 Apr 1954	$8,000[2]	$2,000 p.a.
8 Apr 1963	$12,000 p.a.	$6,000 p.a.
9 Oct 1970	$18,000 p.a.	$8,000—9,650* p.a.
8 Jul 1974	$24,000 p.a.	$10,600—14,475* p.a.

*Depends on area and remoteness of constituency.
[1] If Session exceeds 65 days; otherwise indemnity paid at the rate of $25 per day.
[2] Since 1 Apr 1954 indemnity paid on annual rather than sessional basis.
Note: In addition, all members of the House are entitled to free travel between Ottawa and their constituency or place of residence and (since 1972) up to $9,600 p.a. for the operation of a constituency office.

Senators

Date Effective	Sessional Indemnity	Non-Taxable Expense Allowance
1945	$4,000[1]	$2,000 p.a.
1 Apr 1954	$8,000[2] p.a.	$2,000 p.a.
8 Apr 1963	$12,000 p.a.	$3,000 p.a.
8 Oct 1970	$18,000 p.a.	$4,000 p.a.
8 Jul 1974	$24,000 p.a.	$5,300 p.a.

[1] If Session exceeds 65 days; otherwise indemnity paid at the rate of $25 per day.
[2] Since 1 Apr 1954 indemnity paid on annual rather than sessional basis.
Note: In addition, all Senators are entitled to free travel between Ottawa and their constituency or place of residence.

Office Holders
In all cases, the figures shown are in addition to the pay and allowances of the following members of Parliament.

Prime Minister

Date Effective	Sessional Indemnity
1945[1]	$15,000 + $2,000 auto allowance*
1 Apr 1954[1]	$25,000 + $2,000 auto allowance*
8 Jul 1974	$33,300 + $2,000 auto allowance*

[1] Expense allowance taxable.
*Non-taxable

Cabinet Ministers, Leader of the Opposition

Date Effective	Sessional Indemnity
1945[1]	$10,000 + $2,000 auto allowance*
1 Apr 1954[1]	$15,000 + $2,000 auto allowance*

continued

Date Effective	Sessional Indemnity
8 Jul 1974[2]	$20,000 + $2000 auto allowance*

[1]Expense allowance taxable.
[2]Including Ministers of State.
*Non-taxable.

Ministers Without Portfolio

Date Effective	Sessional Indemnity
1 Apr 1954[1]	$7,500 + $2,000 auto allowance*
8 Jul 1974	$20,000 + $2,000 auto allowance*

[1]Expense allowance taxable.
*Non-taxable.

Speaker of the House of Commons

Date Effective	Sessional Indemnity
1945	$6,000 + $1,000 auto allowance* + $3,000 residence allowance*
1 Apr 1954	$9,000 + $1,000 auto allowance* + $3,000 residence allowance*
8 Jul 1974	$20,000 +$1,000 auto alloance* + $3,000 residence allowance*

*Non-taxable.

Speaker of the Senate

Date Effective	Sessional Indemnity
1945	$6,000 + $1,000 auto allowance* + $3,000 residence allowance*
1 Apr 1954	$6,000 + $1,000 auto allowance* + $3,000 residence allowance*
8 Jul 1974	$12,000 + $1,000 auto allowance* + $3,000 residence allowance*

*Non-taxable.

Deputy Speaker of the House of Commons

Date Effective	Sessional Indemnity
1945	$4,000 + $1,500 in lieu of residence*
1 Apr 1954	$6,000 + $1,500 in lieu of residence*
8 Jul 1974	$8,000 + $1,500 in lieu of residence*

*Non-taxable.

Parliamentary Assistants/Secretaries; Leaders of Recognized Parties;[1] Opposition House Leader, [2] Chief Government and Opposition Whips in Commons,[3] Deputy and Assistant Deputy Chairman of Committees[4]

Date Effective	Sessional Indemnity
1945	$4,000
1 Apr 1954	$4,000
8 Jul 1974	$5,300

[1]Since 8 Apr 1963, recognized party must have 12 or more members in Commons; excludes Prime Minister and Leader of Opposition.
[2]Since 8 Jul 1974.
[3]Since 8 Apr 1963.
[4]Since 8 Jul 1974.

Leader of the Government in the Senate*

Date Effective	Sessional Indemnity
1945	$7,000
1 Apr 1954	$10,000
8 Jul 1974	$13,300

*If not receiving Cabinet Minister's salary.

Deputy Leader of Government in the Senate

Date Effective	Sessional Indemnity
8 Jul 1974	$8,000

Leader of Opposition in the Senate

Date Effective	Sessional Indemnity
1945	$4,000
1 Apr 1954	$6,000
8 Jul 1974	$8,000

Sources: *Canada Year Book 1945 —*; Salaries Act; Senate and House of Commons Act; Parliamentary Secretaries' Act; Governor General's Act.

13. Passage of Legislation in Canada: Pre-Parliamentary and Parliamentary Stages

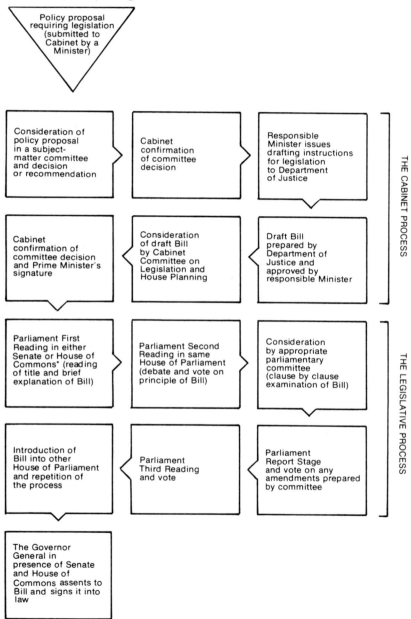

*All money Bills must be introduced in the House of Commons.

Source: *Canada Year Book 1973*, p. 74.

III
ELECTIONS

1. The Franchise in Canada

As of January 1, 1945 the right to vote in Canada was held by all British subjects twenty-one years of age or older ordinarily resident in Canada (and who had been so resident for at least twelve months).* The following, however, were excluded:

1. Judges, Chief and Assistant Chief Electoral Officers, Chief Returning Officers.
2. Lunatics, prisoners and those convicted of corrupt electoral practices.
3. Eskimos, Indians on reservations (unless veterans), inmates of charitable institutions and conscientious objectors if disqualified from voting in the provincial elections of their province of residence.

The following changes have since taken place:

1 Jan 1947 — Canadian citizenship instituted, creating two groups of eligible voters—Canadian citizens and other British subjects ordinarily resident in Canada.
30 Jun 1948 —Exclusion of inmates of charitable institutions repealed.
30 Jun 1950 — Eskimos enfranchised.
11 Jul 1955 — Exclusion of conscientious objectors repealed.
1 Jul 1960 — Indians on reservations enfranchised.
26 Jun 1970 —Voting age reduced to eighteen. Right of British subjects to vote restricted to those qualified as electors on 25 Jun 1968; British subjects to be disenfranchised entirely after a five-year transition period.
25 Jun 1975 —British subjects ordinarily resident in Canada disenfranchised.

*An elector must vote in the electoral district in which he is resident on the date fixed for the beginning of enumeration.
Sources: *Canada Year Book 1945 —*; Canada Election Act and Amendments 1945-1970.

2. General Election Results 1945–1974

	Seats		Votes			
	No.	%	No. '000	%[1]*		'000
1945 Monday, 11 June						
Lib	125	51.0	2,157	41.1	Eligible Voters	– 6,952
PC	67	27.3	1,436	27.4	Votes Cast[2]	– 5,305
CCF	28	11.4	816	15.6	Turnout (%)	– 76%
SC	13	5.3	215	4.1		
Other (includes Bloc	12	4.9	623	11.9		
Populaire, Labour Progressive [Communists] and Independents)						
TOTAL	245					

*Totals may not be exactly 100.0 due to rounding.
[1]Calculation of % ignores spoiled ballots.
[2]Includes spoiled ballots.

1949 Monday, 27 June						
Lib	193	73.7	2,898	49.5	Eligible Voters	– 7,894
PC	41	15.6	1,736	29.7	Votes Cast	– 5,904
CCF	13	5.0	782	13.4	Turnout (%)	– 74%
SC	10	3.8	216	3.7		
Other (Independents)	5	1.9	218	3.7		
TOTAL	262					

continued

	Seats No.	Seats %	Votes No. '000	Votes %[1]*
1953 Monday, 10 August				
Lib	171	64.5	2,788	48.9
PC	51	19.2	1,768	31.0
CCF	23	8.7	644	11.3
SC	15	5.7	308	5.4
Other	5	1.9	194	3.4
TOTAL	265			

'000
Eligible Voters – 8,402
Votes Cast – 5,702
Turnout (%) – 67%

	Seats No.	Seats %	Votes No. '000	Votes %[1]*
1957 Monday, 10 June				
Lib	105	39.6	2,702	40.9
PC	112	42.2	2,573	38.9
CCF	25	9.4	708	10.7
SC	19	7.2	440	6.7
Other	4	1.5	194	2.9
TOTAL	265			

Eligible Voters – 8,902
Votes Cast – 6,681
Turnout (%) – 74%

	Seats No.	Seats %	Votes No. '000	Votes %[1]*
1958 Monday, 31 March				
Lib	49	18.5	2,448	33.6
PC	208	78.5	3,908	53.6
CCF	8	3.0	692	9.5
SC	0	—	188	2.6
Other	0	—	51	0.7
TOTAL	265			

Eligible Voters – 9,131
Votes Cast – 7,357
Turnout (%) – 79%

1962 Monday, 18 June

	Seats	%	Votes	%
Lib	100	37.7	2,847	37.0
PC	116	43.8	2,874	37.4
NDP	19	7.1	1,012	13.2
SC	30	11.3	899	11.7
Other	0	—	97	1.3
TOTAL	265			

Eligible Voters — 9,700
Votes Cast — 7,773
Turnout (%) — 79%

1963 Monday, 8 April

	Seats	%	Votes	%
Lib	129	48.7	3,301	41.8
PC	95	35.8	2,561	32.4
NDP	17	6.4	1,028	13.0
SC	24	9.1	945	12.0
Other	0	—	60	0.8
TOTAL	265			

Eligible Voters — 9,911
Votes Cast — 7,959
Turnout (%) — 79%

1965 Monday, 8 November

	Seats	%	Votes	%
Lib	131	49.4	3,099	40.2
PC	97	36.6	2,500	32.4
NDP	21	7.9	1,382	17.9
SC	5	5.3	642	8.3
RC	9	5.3	642	8.3
Other	2	0.8	92	1.2
TOTAL	265			

Eligible Voters — 10,275
Votes Cast — 7,797
Turnout (%) — 75%

1968 Tuesday, 25 June

	Seats	%	Votes	%
Lib	155	58.7	3,696	45.5
PC	72	27.3	2,554	31.4

Eligible Voters — 10,861
Votes Cast — 8,218

continued

	Seats		Votes			'000
	No.	%	No. '000	%1*		
NDP	22	8.3	1,378	17.0	Turnout (%)	– 76%
RC	14	5.3	361	4.4		
Other	1	0.4	137	1.7		
TOTAL	264					

1972 Monday, 30 October

	No.	%	No. '000	%1*		'000
Lib	109	41.3	3,718	38.5	Eligible Voters	– 13,001
PC	107	40.5	3,384	35.0	Votes Cast	– 9,975
NDP	31	11.7	1,713	17.7	Turnout (%)	– 77%
SC	15	5.7	737	7.6		
Other	2	0.8	113	1.2		
TOTAL	264					

1974 Monday, 8 July

	No.	%	No. '000	%1*		'000
Lib	141	53.4	4,103	43.2	Eligible Voters	– 13,620
PC	95	36.0	3,369	35.4	Votes Cast	– 9,671
NDP	16	6.1	1,468	15.4	Turnout (%)	– 71%
SC	11	4.2	481	5.1		
Other	1	0.4	85	0.9		
TOTAL	264					

Source: Reports of the Chief Electoral Officer, Twentieth to Thirtieth General Elections 1945–1974.

3. General Election Results by Region 1945–1974

	1945	1949	1953	1957	1958	1962	1963	1965	1968	1972	1974
Atlantic											
Lib	19	25	27	12	8	14	20	15	7	10	13
PC	6	7	5	21	25	18	13	18	25	22	17
SC	–	–	–	–	–	–	–	–	–	–	–
CCF–NDP	1	1	1	–	–	1	–	–	–	–	1
Other	1	1	–	–	–	–	–	–	–	–	1
TOTAL	27	34	33	33	33	33	33	33	32	32	32
Quebec											
Lib	53	66	66	63	25	35	47	56	56	56	60
PC	2	2	4	9	50	14	8	8	4	2	3
SC	–	–	–	–	–	26	20	–	–	15	11
Cred	–	–	–	–	–	–	–	9	14	–	–
CCF–NDP	–	–	–	–	–	–	–	–	–	–	–
Other	10	5	5	3	–	–	–	2	–	1	–
TOTAL	65	73	75	75	75	75	75	75	74	74	74
Ontario											
Lib	34	56	50	20	14	43	52	51	64	36	55
PC	48	25	33	61	67	35	27	25	17	40	25
SC	–	–	–	–	–	–	–	–	–	–	–

continued

	1945	1949	1953	1957	1958	1962	1963	1965	1968	1972	1974
CCF–NDP	–	1	1	3	3	6	6	9	6	11	8
Other	–	1	1	1	1	1	–	–	1	1	–
TOTAL	82	83	85	85	85	85	85	85	88	88	88
West*											
Lib	19	43	27	10	1	7	10	9	2	7	13
PC	11	7	9	21	66	49	47	46	26	43	50
SC	13	10	15	19	–	4	4	5	–	–	–
CCF–NDP	27	10	21	22	5	12	11	12	16	20	7
Other	–	–	–	–	–	–	–	–	–	–	–
Total	71	71	72	72	72	72	72	72	70	70	70

*Includes Territories.

Sources: Reports of the Chief Electoral Officer, Twentieth to Thirtieth General Elections 1945 –1974; Canadian Parliamentary Guide 1945 –.

4. House of Commons Seats Won in By-Elections

Year	PC	Lib	CCF−NDP	SC	Other	Number of By-Elections
1945[1]	1	−	−	−	−	1
1945[2]	−	1	−	−	−	1
1946	2	1	−	1	−	4
1947	−	2	−	−	1	3
1948	2	3	4	−	−	9
1949[1]	1	−	−	−	−	1
1949[2]	1	4	−	−	3	8
1950	3	3	−	−	2	8
1951	5	−	−	−	−	5
1952	4	4	−	−	−	8
1954	3	5	1	−	1	10
1955	2	4	−	1	−	7
1957[2]	2	−	−	−	−	2
1958	3	1	−	−	−	4
1959	1	1	−	−	−	2
1960	1	2	1[3]	−	−	4
1961	3	3	−	−	−	4
1962	−	−	1	−	−	1
1964	1	4	1	−	−	6
1966	−	3	−	−	−	3
1967	2	5	1	−	−	8
1968	−	−	1	−	−	1
1969	−	−	2	−	−	2
1970	1	2	1	−	−	4
1971	1	2	2	−	−	5
1975	1	1	−	−	−	2
1976	2	−	−	−	−	2

[1]Before general election.
[2]After general election.
[3]Elected as New Party.

5. House of Commons Seats Changing Hands in By-Elections

Year	PC	Lib	CCF–NDP	SC	Other
1945[1]	+1	−1	−	−	−
1945[2]	−	−	−	−	−
1946	+1	−1	−	+1	−1
1947	−	+1	−	−	−1
1948	−	−2	+3	−	−1
1949[1]	+1	−1	−	−	−
1949[2]	−	−3	−	−	+3
1950	+2	−4	−	−	+2
1951	+2	−2	−	−	−
1952	+3	−3	−	−	−
1954	−	−1	+1	−	−
1955	+2	−2	−	−	−
1957[2]	+1	−1	−	−	−
1960	−2	+1	+1 (NP)	−	−
1961	−1	+1	−	−	−
1962	−	−	−	−	−
1964	−1	−	+1	−	−
1966	−1	+1	−	−	−
1967	−	−1	+1	−	−
1969	−1	−1	+1	−	−
1975	+1	−1	−	−	−
1976	+1	−1	−	−	−

[1]Before general election.
[2]After general election.
Sources: *Reports of the Chief Electoral Officer, By-Elections 1945–1976; Canadian Parliamentary Guide 1945–.*

IV
POLITICAL PARTIES
AND PRESSURE GROUPS

1. Liberal Party of Canada

Liberal Party National Office: 102 Bank Street, Ottawa K1P 5N4, (613) 237-0740

Party Leaders

William Lyon Mackenzie King	1945
Louis S. St. Laurent	7 Aug 1948
Lester B. Pearson	16 Jan 1958
Pierre E. Trudeau	6 Apr 1968

National Party Presidents
(National Liberal Federation/Liberal Party of Canada)

J. Gordon Fogo	1946
Allan Woodrow	1952
Duncan MacTavish	1952
A. Bruce Matthews	1958
Senator John Connolly	1961
Senator J.L. Nichol	1964
Senator Richard Stanbury	6 Apr 1968
Senator Gildas Molgat	16 Sep 1973
Senator Al Graham	9 Nov 1975

Major National Party Conventions and Meetings

Date	Meeting	Location
5–7 Aug 1948	National Leadership Convention	Ottawa
14–16 Jan 1958	National Leadership Convention	Ottawa
6–10 Sep 1960	Study Conference on National Problems	Kingston
9–11 Jan 1961	National Policy Convention	Ottawa
9–11 Oct 1966	National Policy Convention	Ottawa
4–6 Apr 1968	National Leadership Convention	Ottawa
20–23 Nov 1969	"Thinkers" Policy Conference	Harrison Hot Springs, B.C.
20–22 Nov 1970	National Policy Convention	Ottawa
14–16 Sep 1973	National Convention	Ottawa
7–9 Nov 1975	National Policy Convention	Ottawa
24–27 Mar 1977	National Liberal Workshop	Toronto

Leadership Convention Results
(In each case balloting held on final day of convention.)

Candidate	First	Second	Ballot Third	Fourth
5−7 August 1948				
James Gardiner	323			
C.G. Power	56			
Louis St. Laurent	848			
TOTAL	1227			
14−16 January 1958				
L. Henderson	1			
Paul Martin	305			
Lester B. Pearson	1074			
TOTAL	1380			
4−6 April 1968				
J.J. Greene	169	104	29*	
Paul Hellyer	330	465	377**	
L. Henderson	0*			
Eric Kierans	103**			
Allan MacEachen	165	11***		
Paul Martin	277**			
Pierre E. Trudeau	752	964	1051	1203
John Turner	277	347	279	195
Robert Winters	293	473	621	954
TOTAL	2366	2364	2357	2352

* Eliminated after this ballot.
** Withdrew after this ballot.
*** Withdrew after first ballot but failed to notify convention chairman in time to have name removed from second ballot; formally eliminated after second ballot.

2. **Progressive Conservative Party of Canada**

Progressive Conservative Party National Headquarters: 178 Queen Street, Ottawa K1P 5E1, (613) 238-6111

Party Leaders

John Bracken	1945
George Drew	2 Oct 1948
John G. Diefenbaker	14 Dec 1956
Robert L. Stanfield	9 Sep 1967
Joe Clark	21 Feb 1976

National Party Presidents

(Progressive Conservative Association of Canada)

Peter MacArthur	1945
J.M. Macdonnell	29 Mar 1946
George Nowlan	19 Apr 1950
George Hees	17 Mar 1954
Léon Balcer	18 Jan 1956
Senator G. Thorvaldson	2 Dec 1959
Egan Chambers	19 Jan 1963
Dalton Camp	5 Feb 1964
Frank Moores	12 Mar 1969
Nathan Nurgitz	20 Jun 1970
Donald J. Matthews	8 Dec 1971
Michael Meighen	19 Mar 1974

Major National Party Conventions and Meetings

Date	Meeting	Location
30 Sep–2 Oct 1948	National Leadership Convention	Ottawa
12–14 Dec 1956	National Leadership Convention	Ottawa
13–16 Nov 1966	Annual Meeting, PC Association of Canada — decision taken to hold 1967 leadership convention	Ottawa
7–10 Aug 1967	Policy Advisory Conference	Montmorency Falls, P.Q.
5–9 Sep 1967	National Leadership Convention	Toronto
9–13 Oct 1969	National Policy Convention	Niagara Falls
6–7 Dec 1971	National Policy Convention	Ottawa
17–19 Mar 1974	National Convention	Ottawa
19–22 Feb 1976	National Leadership Convention	Ottawa

Leadership Convention Results
(In each case balloting held on final day of convention.)

			Ballot		
Candidate	First	Second	Third	Fourth	Fifth
30 Sep−2 Oct 1948					
John G. Diefenbaker	311				
George Drew	827				
Donald M. Fleming	104				
TOTAL	1242				
12−14 Dec 1956					
John G. Diefenbaker	774				
Donald M. Fleming	393				
E. Davie Fulton	117				
TOTAL	1284				
5−9 Sep 1967					
John G. Diefenbaker	271	172	114*		
Donald M. Fleming	126	115	76**		
E. Davie Fulton	343	346	361	357*	
Alvin Hamilton	136	127	106	167**	
George Hees	295	299	277*		
John MacLean	10*				
Wallace McCutcheon	137	76*			
Duff Roblin	347	430	541	771	969
Robert L. Stanfield	519	613	717	865	1150
Michael Starr	45	34**			
Mary Walker-Sawka	2**				
TOTAL	2231	2212	2192	2160	2119
19−22 Feb 1976					
Joseph Clark	277	532	969	1187	
John Fraser	127	34**			
James Gillies	87*				
Howard Grafftey	33**				
Paul Hellyer	231	118*			
Jack Horner	235	286*			
Flora Macdonald	214	239*			

continued

Candidate	First	Second	Ballot Third	Fourth	Fifth
Brian Mulroney	357	419	369**		
Patrick Nowlan	86	42*			
Richard Quittenton***					
Sinclair Stevens	182*				
Claude Wagner	531	667	1003	1122	
TOTAL	2360	2337	2341	2309	

*Withdrew after this ballot.
**Eliminated after this ballot.
***Withdrew before first ballot.

3. Co-operative Commonwealth Federation/New Democratic Party of Canada

NDP National Office: 301 Metcalf Street, Ottawa K2P 1R9, (613) 236-3613

Party Leaders

CCF

M. J. Coldwell	1945
Hazen Argue	11 Aug 1960

NDP

T. C. Douglas	4 Aug 1961
David Lewis	24 Apr 1971
Edward Broadbent	7 Jul 1975

National Party Chairman (CCF)

F. R. Scott	1945
Percy Wright	28 Jul 1950
David Lewis	30 Jul 1954

National Party President (NDP)

Michael Oliver	4 Aug 1961
Eamon Park	15 Jul 1965
James Renwick	5 Jul 1967
Allan Blakeney	29 Oct 1969
Donald Macdonald	23 Apr 1971
Joyce Nash	7 Jul 1975

Major National Party Conventions and Meetings

Both the CCF and the NDP have always held biennial national party conventions at which the leadership must be reviewed and at which the incumbent may be challenged. The following is a list of biennial conventions and indicates those which produced a change of leadership.

Date	Place
CCF	
7−9 Aug 1946	Regina
19−21 Aug 1949	Winnipeg
26−28 Jul 1950	Vancouver
6−8 Aug 1952	Toronto
28−30 Jul 1954	Edmonton
1−3 Aug 1956	Winnipeg
23−25 July 1958	Montreal
9−11 Aug 1960	Regina (Leadership convention)
NDP	
31 Jul−4 Aug 1961	Ottawa (Founding convention of NDP and leadership convention)
6−9 Aug 1963	Regina
12−15 Jul 1965	Toronto
3−6 Jul 1967	Toronto
29−31 Oct 1969	Winnipeg
21−24 Apr 1971	Ottawa (Leadership convention)
19−22 Jul 1973	Vancouver
4−7 Jul 1975	Winnipeg (Leadership convention)

Leadership Convention Results
(In each case balloting held on final day of convention.)

		Ballot		
Candidate	First	Second	Third	Fourth
9−11 Aug 1960				
Hazen Argue elected unanimously without contest.				
31 Jul−4 Aug 1961				
Hazen Argue	380			
T. C. Douglas	1391			
TOTAL	1771			
21−24 Apr 1971				
Ed Broadbent	236	223*		
John Harney	299	347	431*	
Frank Howard	124*			
James Laxer	378	407	508	612
David Lewis	661	715	742	1046
TOTAL	1698	1692	1681	1658

continued

| Candidate | | Ballot | | |
	First	Second	Third	Fourth
4 −7 Jul 1975				
Ed Broadbent	536	586	694	984
Rosemary Brown	413	397	494	658
Douglas Campbell	11*			
John Harney	313	299*		
Lorne Nystrom	345	342	413*	
TOTAL	1618	1624	1601	1642

*Eliminated after this ballot.

4. Social Credit Party of Canada

Address: P.O. Box 1391, Station B, Ottawa K1P 5R4, (613) 235-0583

Party Leaders

National Leader

Solon Low	1945
Robert Thompson	6 Jul 1961
A. B. Patterson (Acting)	17 Mar 1967
Vacant	
Réal Caouette	11 Oct 1971
André Fortin	7 Nov 1976

Associate Leader

Réal Caouette	6 Jul 1961−31 Aug 1963

Ralliement Créditiste/Social Credit Rally

The Ralliement Créditiste was organized in August 1958 as the Quebec wing of the Social Credit Party, uniting elements of the Union des Electeurs and the Vers Demain movements under the leadership of Réal Caouette. In August 1963 the Ralliement Créditiste split from the Social Credit Party, electing Caouette as leader. In October 1968 the party was renamed the Ralliement Créditiste/Social Credit Rally as one of a number of overtures to Anglophone Social Crediters. The RC/SCR was formally reunited with the remnants of the Social Credit Party under its name in April 1971 at a National Council of Social Crediters' meeting in Ottawa. A leadership convention was held in October 1971.

National Party Presidents

Solon Low	1945 (United with office of national leader, 1945–1960)
Robert Thompson	30 Jul 1960
Martin Kelln	6 Jul 1961
Herbert Bruch	17 Mar 1967
Gilbert Rondeau	Apr 1971
Martin J. Hattersley	2 Sept 1973

Major National Party Conventions and Meetings

Date	Meeting	Location
28–30 Jul 1960	National Convention	Ottawa
4–6 Jul 1961	National Leadership Convention	Ottawa
29 Aug–1 Sept 1963	Convention of Ralliement Créditiste	Granby, P.Q.
Apr 1971	National Council of Social Crediters	Ottawa
9–11 Oct 1971	National Leadership Convention	Hull, P.Q.
6–7 Nov 1976	National Leadership Convention	Ottawa

Leadership Convention Results

(In each case balloting held on final day of convention.)

	Ballot	
Candidates	First	Second

4–6 Jul 1961
Réal Caouette
George Hahn
A. B. Patterson
R. N. Thompson
R. N. Thompson elected leader on first ballot, but actual results never made public. Caouette unanimously named associate leader.

30 Aug 1963
Caouette unanimously elected leader of the Ralliement Créditiste in uncontested election.

9–11 Oct 1971

Fernand Bourret	9	
Réal Caouette	510	

continued

Candidates	Ballot	
	First	Second
Phil Cossette	104	
James McGillivray	69	
TOTAL	692	
6–7 Nov 1976		
Alex Barker	3	
Ralph Cameron	48	
André Fortin	532	610
Martin Hattersley	194	165
Philip Hele-Hambly	18	
John Long	31	
René Matte	317	317
TOTAL	1143	1092

5. Union Nationale Party

The Union Nationale, which participates only in Quebec provincial politics, was formed in June 1936 by the merger of the Quebec Conservative Party and a group of dissident Liberals known as L'Action Libérale Nationale under the inspiration and leadership of Maurice Duplessis, leader since 1933 of the Quebec Conservative Party.

Between October 1971 and January 1973, the party's name was changed to Unité-Québec. On 1 June 1975 the party absorbed the Parti Présidentiel, a group composed of dissident Créditistes.

Party Leaders

Maurice Duplessis	1945
Vacant	7 Sep 1959
Paul Sauvé	11 Sep 1959
Vacant	2 Jan 1960
Antonio Barrette	8 Jan 1960
Yves Prévost	3 Oct 1960 (Interim Leader)
Antonio Talbot	12 Jan 1961 (Interim Leader)
Daniel Johnson	23 Sep 1961
Vacant	26 Sep 1968
Jean-Jacques Bertrand	2 Oct 1968 (Interim Leader)
Jean-Jacques Bertrand	21 Jun 1969
Gabriel Loubier	19 Jun 1971
Maurice Bellemare	30 Mar 1974 (Interim Leader)
Rodrique Biron	23 May 1976

Major Party Conventions

Date	Location
21–23 Sep 1961	Quebec City
19–21 Jun 1969	Quebec City
17–19 Jun 1971	Quebec City
11–23 May 1976	Quebec City

Leadership Convention Results

(In each case balloting held on final day of convention.)

		Ballots	
Candidate	First	Second	Third
21–23 Sep 1961			
Jean-Jacques Bertrand	912		
Daniel Johnson	1006		
Raymond Maher	2		
Armand Nadeau	24		
TOTAL	1944		
19–21 Jun 1969			
Jean-Jacques Bertrand	1325		
Jean-Guy Cardinal	938		
Andre Léveillé	22		
TOTAL	2285		
17–19 Jun 1971			
Mario Beaulieu	178	99*	
Andre Léveillé	0*		
Gabriel Loubier	529	568	607
Marcel Masse	482	544	584
Pierre Sévigny	26*		
TOTAL	1215	1211	1191

* Eliminated after this ballot.

Candidate	First	Second	Third
21–23 May 1976			
Rodrique Biron	764		
Jean-Guy LaBoeuf	103		
Gerard Nepveu	123		
William Shaw	60		
Jacques Tetrault	270		
TOTAL	1320		

6. Parti Québecois

The Parti Québecois, a separatist party which participates only in Quebec provincial politics, has its origins in several earlier separatist groups. The most important of these were Le Rassemblement pour L'Indépendance Nationale (RIN), formed in 1960, and Le Ralliement National (RN), formed in 1966. When René Lévesque resigned from the Quebec Liberal Party, he was instrumental in the establishment of the Mouvement Souveraineté-Association (MSA) in November 1967 for the purpose of uniting all groups seeking an independent Quebec. In March 1968 the RIN agreed to form a common front with the MSA, and in August 1968 the RN agreed to unite with the MSA. The MSA organized the founding convention of the Parti Québecois in Quebec City, 11–14 October 1968. Shortly afterwards, on 24 October 1968, the RIN agreed to unite with the PQ.

Party Leaders

René Lévesque	14 Oct 1968

Party President

René Lévesque	14 Oct 1968

Major Party Conventions

Date	Place
11–14 Oct 1968	Quebec City
17–19 Oct 1969	Montreal
26–28 Feb 1971	Quebec City
23–25 Feb 1973	Montreal
16–17 Nov 1974	Quebec City

7. Pressure/Interest Groups in Canada

Business and Agriculture
Canadian Federation of Agriculture
National Farmers' Union
National Dairy Council of Canada
Canadian Manufacturers' Association
Canadian Chamber of Commerce
Canadian Bankers' Association
National Association of Canadian Credit Unions
Mining Association of Canada
Life Underwriters' Association of Canada

Canadian Construction Association
Association of Canadian Advertisers
Pharmaceutical Manufacturers' Association of Canada

Labour
Canadian Labour Congress
Confederation of National Trade Unions

Professions
Canadian Medical Association
Canadian Bar Association
Canadian Association of University Teachers
Canadian Teachers' Federation
Canadian Nurses' Association

Education and Public Administration
Association of Universities and Colleges of Canada
Canadian Home and School and Parent-Teacher Federation
National Union of Students
Union Générale des Etudiants du Québec
Civil Service Federation of Canada
Canadian Association of Chiefs of Police
Institute of Public Administration of Canada
Canadian Federation of Mayors and Municipalities

Media
Canadian Daily Newspaper Publishers' Association
Canadian Association of Broadcasters

Groups Concerned with Special Segments of the Populace

Veterans
Royal Canadian Legion
Army, Navy and Air Force Veterans of Canada

Women
Canadian Federation of University Women
Canadian Women's Club
National Council of Women in Canada
Canadian Federation of Business and Professional Women's Clubs

Ethnic/Patriotic
Société St. Jean-Baptiste
Imperial Order Daughters of the Empire

Native Sons of Canada
Loyal Orange Association
Empire Club of Canada

Religious
Canadian Catholic Conference
Canadian Council of Churches
Catholic Women's League of Canada
Knights of Columbus
Canadian Jewish Congress
Student Christian Movement of Canada

Groups Concerned with Special Causes and Social and Political Action
United Nations Association in Canada
Committee for an Independent Canada
Canadian Peace Congress
Voice of Women
Canadian Civil Liberties Association
Consumers' Association of Canada
Canadian Red Cross Society
Canadian Council of Christians and Jews
Canadian Council on Social Development
Canadian Mental Health Association
Pollution Probe
Canadian Wildlife Federation

V
THE JUDICIARY

1. Chief Justice of the Supreme Court of Canada

T. Rinfret	1945–21 Jun 1954
P. Kerwin	1 Jul 1954–2 Feb 1963
R. Taschereau	22 Apr 1963–31 Aug 1967
J. R. Cartwright	1 Sep 1967–22 Mar 1970
G. Fauteux	23 Mar 1970–22 Dec 1973
B. Laskin	27 Dec 1973–

2. Justices of the Supreme Court of Canada

	Years on Supreme Court
T. Rinfret	1924–1954
P. Kerwin	1935–1963
A. B. Hudson	1936–1946
R. Taschereau	1940–1967
I. C. Rand	1943–1959
R. L. Kellock	1944–1958
J. W. Estey	1944–1955
C. H. Locke	1947–1961
J. R. Cartwright	1949–1970
G. Fauteux	1949–1973
D. C. Abbott	1954–1974
H. G. Nolan	1956–1957
R. Martland	1958–
W. Judson	1958–
R. A. Ritchie	1959–
E. M. Hall	1962–1973
W. F. Spence	1963–
L. P. Pigeon	1967–
B. Laskin	1970–
R. G. B. Dickson	1973–
J. Beetz	1974–
L. P. De Grandpré	1974–

3. President of the Exchequer Court of Canada

J.T. Thorson	1945–3 May 1964
W. R. Jackett	4 May 1964–31 May 1971

(Reorganized as Federal Court of Canada 1 Jun 1971.)

4. Chief Justice of the Federal Court of Canada

W. R. Jackett	1 Jun 1971–

Source: *Canada Year Book 1945 –* .

5. The Canadian Judicial System

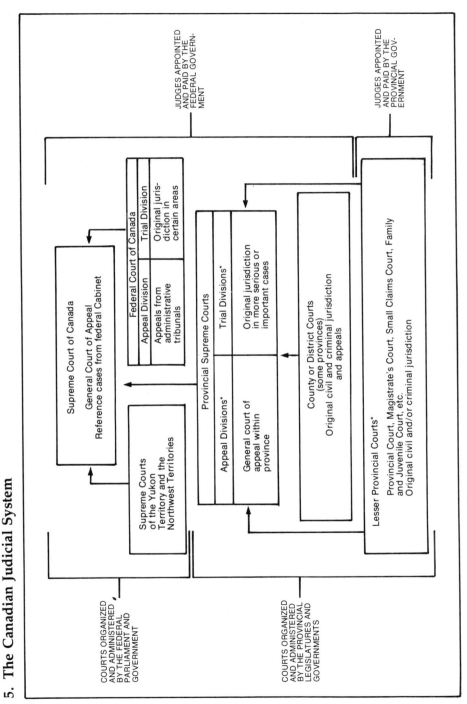

*Names of courts vary from province to province.

VI
THE PROVINCES AND
FEDERAL-PROVINCIAL RELATIONS

1. Provincial Governments

Premier	Date of Appointment	Party
Newfoundland		
Joseph R. Smallwood	1 Apr 1949	Lib
Frank D. Moores	18 Jan 1972	PC
Prince Edward Island		
J. Walter Jones	1945	Lib
A.W. Matheson	25 May 1953	Lib
Walter Shaw	1 Sep 1959	PC
Alexander B. Campbell	28 Jul 1966	Lib
Nova Scotia		
A.S. MacMillan	1945	Lib
Angus L. Macdonald	8 Sep 1945	Lib
Harold Connolly	13 Apr 1954	Lib
Henry D. Hicks	30 Sep 1954	Lib
Robert L. Stanfield	20 Nov 1956	PC
George I. Smith	13 Sep 1967	PC
Gerald Regan	28 Oct 1970	Lib
New Brunswick		
J. B. McNair	1945	Lib
H. J. Flemming	8 Oct 1952	PC
L. J. Robichaud	12 Jul 1960	Lib
Richard B. Hatfield	12 Nov 1970	PC
Quebec		
Maurice Duplessis	1945	Union Nationale
Paul Sauvé	10 Sep 1959	Union Nationale
Antonio Barrette	7 Jan 1960	Union Nationale
Jean Lesage	5 Jul 1960	Lib
Daniel Johnson	16 Jun 1966	Union Nationale
Jean Jacques Bertrand	2 Oct 1968	Union Nationale
Robert Bourassa	12 May 1970	Lib
René Lévesque	25 Nov 1976	Parti Québecois
Ontario		
George Drew	1945	PC
T. L. Kennedy	19 Oct 1948	PC
Leslie M. Frost	4 May 1949	PC
John Robarts	8 Nov 1961	PC
William G. Davis	1 Mar 1971	PC

continued

Premier	Date of Appointment	Party
Manitoba		
S. S. Garson	1945	Coalition
D. L. Campbell	7 Nov 1948	Lib
Dufferin Roblin	16 Jun 1958	PC
Walter C. Weir	27 Nov 1967	PC
Edward R. Shreyer	15 Jul 1969	NDP
Saskatchewan		
T. C. Douglas	1945	CCF
S. Lloyd	7 Nov 1961	CCF-NDP
Ross Thatcher	30 Jun 1964	Lib
Allan Blakeney	30 Jun 1971	NDP
Alberta		
E. C. Manning	1945	SC
Harry E. Strom	12 Dec 1968	SC
Peter Lougheed	10 Sept 1971	PC
British Columbia		
John Hart	1945	Coalition (Lib-PC)
Byron Johnson/		
Herbert Anscomb	29 Dec 1947	Coalition (Lib-PC)
Byron Johnson	18 Jan 1952	Coalition (Lib-PC)
W. A. C. Bennett	1 Aug 1952	SC
David Barrett	30 Aug 1972	NDP
William Bennett	22 Dec 1975	SC

2. Provincial Election Results

Election Date	Result				Size of Legislature
	PC	Lib	CCF-NDP	Other	
Newfoundland					
27 May 1949	5	22	—	1	28
26 Nov 1951	4	24	—	—	28
2 Oct 1956	4	32	—	—	36
20 Aug 1959	3	31	—	2	36
19 Nov 1962	8	34	—	—	42
8 Sep 1966	3	39	—	—	42
28 Oct 1971	21	20	—	1	42
24 Mar 1972	33	9	—	—	42
16 Sep 1975	30	16	—	5*	51

*Includes 4 Liberal Reform Party.

continued

Election Date	PC	Lib	CCF-NDP	Other	Size of Legislature
Prince Edward Island					
11 Dec 1947	6	24	—	—	30
26 Apr 1951	6	24	—	—	30
25 May 1955	3	27	—	—	30
1 Sep 1959	22	8	—	—	30
10 Dec 1962	19	11	—	—	30
30 May 1966	15	17	—	—	32
11 May 1970	5	27	—	—	32
29 Apr 1974	6	26	—	—	32
Nova Scotia					
23 Oct 1945	—	28	2	—	30
9 Jun 1949	7	28	2	—	37
26 May 1953	13	22	2	—	37
30 Oct 1956	24	18	1	—	43
8 Jun 1960	27	15	1	—	43
8 Oct 1963	39	4	—	—	43
30 May 1967	40	6	—	—	46
13 Oct 1970	21	23	2	—	46
2 Apr 1974	12	31	3	—	46
New Brunswick					
28 Jun 1948	5	47	—	—	52
22 Sep 1952	36	16	—	—	52
18 Jun 1956	37	15	—	—	52
27 Jun 1960	21	31	—	—	52
22 Apr 1963	20	32	—	—	52
23 Oct 1967	26	32	—	—	58
26 Oct 1970	31	27	—	—	58
18 Nov 1974	33	25	—	—	58
Ontario					
4 Jun 1945	66	11	8	5	90
7 Jun 1948	53	13	21	3	90
22 Nov 1951	79	7	2	2	90
9 Jun 1955	84	11	3	—	98
11 Jun 1959	71	22	5	—	98
25 Sep 1963	77	24	7	—	108
17 Oct 1967	69	28	20	—	117
21 Oct 1971	78	20	19	—	117
18 Sep 1975	51	36	38	—	125

Election Date	PC	Lib	CCF-NDP	SC	Other	Size of Legislature
Manitoba						
15 Oct 1945	13	26	10	2	4	55

continued

			Result			Size of
Election Date	PC	Lib	CCF-NDP	SC	Other	Legislature
10 Nov 1949	10	29	7	—	11	57
8 Jun 1953	12	35	5	2	3	57
16 Jun 1958	26	19	11	—	1	57
14 May 1959	36	11	10	1	—	57
14 Dec 1962	36	13	7	1	—	57
23 Jun 1966	31	14	11	1	—	57
25 Jun 1969	22	5	28	1	1	57
28 Jun 1973	21	5	31	—	—	57

Saskatchewan

24 Jun 1948	—	19	31	—	2	52
11 Jun 1952	—	11	42	—	—	53
20 Jun 1956	—	14	36	3	—	53
8 Jun 1960	—	17	38	—	—	55
22 Apr 1964	1	33	25	—	—	59
11 Oct 1967	—	35	24	—	—	59
23 Jun 1971	—	15	45	—	—	60
23 Jun 1975	7	15	39	—	—	61

Alberta

17 Aug 1948	—	3	2	50	2	57
5 Aug 1952	2	4	2	52	1	61
29 Jun 1955	3	15	—	37	5	61
18 Jun 1959	1	1	—	62	1	65
17 Jun 1963	—	2	—	60	1	63
24 May 1967	6	3	—	55	1	65
30 Aug 1971	49	—	1	25	—	75
26 Mar 1975	69	—	1	4	1	75

British Columbia

25 Oct 1945	37 (Lib-PC Coalition)		10	—	1	48
15 Jun 1949	39 (Lib-PC Coalition)		7	—	2	48
12 Jun 1952	4	6	18	19	1	48
9 Jun 1953	1	4	14	28	1	48
19 Sep 1956	—	2	10	39	1	52
12 Sep 1960	—	4	16	32	—	52
30 Sep 1963	—	5	14	33	—	52
12 Sep 1966	—	6	16	33	—	55
27 Aug 1969	—	5	11	39	—	55
30 Aug 1972	2	5	38	10	—	55
11 Dec 1975	1	1	18	35	—	55

continued

| Election Date | Results | | | | | Size of Legislature |
	Lib	UN	PQ	SC	Other	
Quebec						
28 Jul 1948	8	82	–	–	2	92
16 Jul 1952	23	68	–	–	1	92
20 Jun 1956	19	73	–	–	1	93
22 Jun 1960	51	43	–	–	1	95
14 Nov 1962	63	31	–	–	1	95
5 Jun 1966	50	56	–	–	2	108
29 Apr 1970	72	17	7	12	–	108
29 Oct 1973	102	–	6	2	–	110
15 Nov 1976	28	11	69	1	1	110

3. Federal-Provincial Plenary Conferences of Premiers and Prime Ministers

Date	Location	Subject
6–10 Aug 1945 ⎱ 27 Apr 1946 ⎰	Ottawa	Post-war reconstruction
4–7 Dec 1950	Ottawa	Patriation of B.N.A. Act, finances, pensions
3–6 Oct 1955	Ottawa	Federal-provincial financial relations
25–26 Nov 1957	Ottawa	Federal-provincial financial relations
25–27 Jul 1960	Ottawa	Federal-provincial financial relations
23–24 Feb 1961	Ottawa	Federal-provincial financial relations
26–27 Jul 1963	Ottawa	Pensions, Municipal Loan Fund
26–29 Nov 1963	Ottawa	Pensions, constitutional reform, federal-provincial financial relations
31 Mar– 2 Apr 1964	Quebec City	Pensions, federal-provincial finances
24–28 Oct 1966	Ottawa	Post-secondary education financing, federal-provincial finances
5–7 Feb 1968	Ottawa	Constitutional reform
10–12 Feb 1969	Ottawa	Constitutional reform
8–10 Dec 1969	Ottawa	Constitutional reform

continued

Date	Location	Subject
16–17 Feb 1970	Ottawa	Inflation
16 Sep 1970	Ottawa	The economy
14–18 Jun 1971	Victoria	Constitutional reform — Victoria Charter proposal
23–25 May 1973	Ottawa	Health and post-secondary education financing
22–23 Jan 1974	Ottawa	Energy problems and policy
30 Oct 1974	Ottawa	The economy
9–10 Apr 1975	Ottawa	Energy policy and pricing
6 May 1976	Ottawa	Energy policy and pricing
14–15 Jun 1976	Ottawa	Federal-provincial finances, patriation of B.N.A. Act.
13–14 Dec 1976	Ottawa	Federal-provincial finances

Sources, *Canada Year Book 1945–*; *Canadian News Facts 1975, 1976.*

4. Interprovincial Conferences (Provincial Premiers and Prime Ministers)

Date	Location
1–2 Dec 1960	Quebec
14–15 Aug 1961	Charlottetown
6–7 Aug 1962	Victoria
5–6 Aug 1963	Halifax
3–5 Aug 1964	Jasper Alta.
2–3 Aug 1965	Winnipeg
1–2 Aug 1966	Toronto
1–2 Aug 1967	Fredericton
27–30 Nov 1967	Toronto (Confederation of Tomorrow Conference)
1–2 Aug 1968	Waskesiu, Sask.
4–5 Aug 1969	Quebec City
3–4 Aug 1970	Winnipeg
5–6 Aug 1971	Victoria
3–4 Aug 1972	Halifax
9–10 Aug 1973	Charlottetown
12–13 Sep 1974	Toronto
18–22 Aug 1975	St. John's
18–20 Aug 1976	Banff, Alta.
1–2 Oct 1976	Toronto (Constitutional amendment and patriation)

Sources: *Canada Year Book 1961–*; *Canadian News Facts 1976.*

5. Major Conditional Grant/ Shared Cost Programs

Conditional Grant Program	Years in Effect	Federal Contribution Fiscal 1976/7 (Est.) ($ Million)
Health		
Venereal Disease	1919–1953	
Health Facilities Survey	1948–1953	
Hospital Construction	1948–1970	
Professional Training	1948–	2.3
Crippled Children	1948–1960	
Mental Health	1948–1972	
Tuberculosis Control	1948–1972	
Public Health Research	1948–1972	
Cancer Control	1948–1972	
General Public Health	1948–1972	
Medical Rehabilitation	1953–1972	
Child and Maternal Health	1953–1972	
Health Resources Fund	1966–	36.8
Hospital Insurance	1958–	2,837.4
Medicare	1968–	954.2
Welfare		
Old Age Pensions	1927–1952	
Old Age Assistance*	1952–1966	
Blind Persons Assistance*	1952–1966	
Disabled Persons Assistance*	1954–1966	
Unemployment Assistance*	1956–1966	
Canada Assistance Plan	1966–	1,396.2

* Largely absorbed by Canada Assistance Plan since 1966; these programs will be phased out completely by 1981 though small residual payments are still being made to some provinces.

Education

Vocational Training Assistance	1942–1967[2]	
Post-Secondary Education Assistance[1]	1967– [3]	1,491.1

[1] As of 1 April 1977 separate federal contributions for the hospital insurance, medicare and post-secondary education assistance programs have been replaced by a transfer of 13.5 personal and 1 corporate income tax points to the provinces and a single cash payment. Estimated size of this cash payment for the 1977–78 fiscal year is $2,811.3 million.

continued

Conditional Grant Program	Years in Effect	Federal Contribution Fiscal 1976/7 (Est.) ($ Million)

[2] This program was substantially altered and enlarged in 1960 and terminated in 1967. However, phase-out payments continued for several years thereafter.
[3] Strictly speaking this program is not a conditional grant scheme but it is similar to one. Its size and importance justify its inclusion in this listing.

Resource Development

Forestry Development (several programs)	1951/7–1962	
Comprehensive Forest Development Program	1962–	*
Roads to Resources	1958–	*
Agricultural Programs	1912–	*

* Included in total for DREE.

Regional Development

Agricultural Rehabilitation and Development Programs (ARDA)	1961–	114.4
Fund for Rural Economic Development (FRED)	1966–	
DREE		253.7*

* Includes remaining resource and development programs.

Others

Trans-Canada Highway	1950–1972	
Bilingualism Development	1972–	130.3
Municipal Winter Works	1958–1969	

Sources: *Canada Year Book 1945 – ; Federal-Provincial Programs and Activities 1975*, Ottawa: Federal-Provincial Relations Office, 1975; *How Your Tax Dollar is Spent 1976–7*, Ottawa: Treasury Board, 1976.

6. Equalization Payments to the Provinces Fiscal Years Ending 31 March 1958 to 1977
($ Million)

	Nfld.	P.E.I.	N.S.	N.B.	P.Q.	Ont.	Man.	Sask.	Alta.	B.C.	Total
1958	11.6	3.0	17.4	8.6	43.1	—	19.2	19.2	14.7	4.5	136.0
1959	12.2	3.1	15.6	8.7	55.0	—	12.9	19.9	8.0	8.2	143.4
1960	14.3	3.0	20.7	16.9	68.6	—	13.0	20.2	15.1	11.3	183.0
1961	15.4	3.5	21.0	17.4	70.4	—	14.1	23.7	17.5	5.9	188.9
1962	11.2	2.8	18.2	16.0	62.6	—	11.9	21.2	14.9	5.9	164.7
1963	13.5	3.1	19.5	15.5	77.8	—	15.2	27.6	8.1	-3.7	176.6
1964	15.0	3.8	19.1	16.5	70.2	—	13.6	22.4	6.8	—	167.4
1965	18.4	5.5	26.2	22.9	103.1	—	21.6	24.1	4.8	—	226.6
1966	22.2	6.0	35.5	35.7	125.2	—	25.3	26.7	.5	-2.1	275.0
1967	29.0	7.2	41.6	35.1	155.5	—	32.6	34.3	.3	-.2	335.5
1968	65.2	13.6	70.6	62.2	229.4	—	41.0	21.9	1.6	—	505.4
1969	72.7	14.2	83.6	74.9	284.0	—	40.4	18.8	—	—	588.7
1970*	86.0	16.9	90.0	83.1	343.1	—	42.1	12.3	—	—	673.5
1971	93.7	21.9	90.3	79.9	450.0	—	52.3	42.1	—	—	927.0
1972	120.6	23.2	93.8	97.2	511.6	—	58.6	115.6	—	—	1,020.5
1973	114.4	25.1	146.8	125.2	462.4	—	89.8	173.6	—	—	1,137.4
1974*	157.1	35.2	178.3	151.0	664.1	—	104.7	141.6	—	—	1,432.4
1975*	176.0	40.0	198.3	172.7	727.8	—	112.7	142.8	—	—	1,570.3
1976*	203.4	48.7	243.2	217.1	1,033.4	—	124.4	115.4	—	—	1,985.6
1977*	224.0	53.7	285.6	228.7	1,093.5	—	157.6	101.9	—	—	2,145.0
1978*	269.3	70.3	349.5	275.6	1,262.3	—	200.9	39.1	—	—	2,467.0

* Estimate.
Sources: *House of Commons Debates*, 18 February 1970, p. 3744; *How Your Tax Dollar Is Spent*, Ottawa: Treasury Board, 1974–5; 1975–6; 1976–7; *Canada Year Book 1973–*.

VII
THE CANADIAN ECONOMY

1. Gross National Product

Year	($ Million) Market Prices	Constant (1971) Dollars
1945	11,863	29,071
1946	11,885	28,292
1947	13,473	29,498
1948	15,509	30,231
1949	16,800	31,388
1950	18,491	33,762
1951	21,640	35,450
1952	24,588	38,617
1953	25,833	40,605
1954	25,918	40,106
1955	28,528	43,891
1956	32,058	47,599
1957	33,513	48,718
1958	34,777	49,844
1959	36,846	51,737
1960	38,359	53,231
1961	39,646	54,741
1962	42,927	58,475
1963	45,978	61,487
1964	50,280	65,610
1965	55,364	69,981
1966	61,828	74,844
1967	66,409	77,344
1968	72,586	81,864
1969	79,815	86,225
1970	85,685	88,390
1971	94,115	94,115
1972	104,669	99,680
1973	122,582	106,845
1974	144,616	110,293
1975	161,132	110,975
1976	184,500	n.a.

Source: Statistics Canada, *National Income and Expenditure Accounts.*

2. Canada's Trade Balance (Current Account)

Year	Merchandise Balance	($ Million) Non-Merchandise Balance	Balance of Payments (Current Account)
1945	+ 2,032	− 1,343	+ 689
1946	+ 571	− 208	+ 363
1947	+ 188	− 139	+ 49
1948	+ 432	+ 19	+ 451
1949	+ 293	− 116	+ 177
1950	+ 7	− 326	− 319
1951	− 151	− 361	− 512
1952	+ 485	− 298	+ 187
1953	− 60	− 388	− 448
1954	+ 18	− 442	− 422
1955	− 211	− 476	− 687
1956	− 728	− 644	− 1,372
1957	− 594	− 857	− 1,451
1958	− 176	− 961	− 1,137
1959	− 421	− 1,066	− 1,487
1960	− 148	− 1,085	− 1,233
1961	+ 173	− 1,101	− 928
1962	+ 184	− 1,014	− 830
1963	+ 503	− 1,024	− 521
1964	+ 701	− 1,125	− 424
1965	+ 118	− 1,248	− 1,130
1966	+ 224	− 1,386	− 1,162
1967	+ 566	− 1,065	− 499
1968	+ 1,471	− 1,568	− 97
1969	+ 964	− 1,881	− 917
1970	+ 3,052	− 1,946	+ 1,106
1971	+ 2,563	− 2,132	+ 431
1972	+ 1,857	− 2,243	− 386
1973	+ 2,735	− 2,639	+ 96
1974	+ 1,698	− 3,190	− 1,492
1975	− 639	− 4,326	− 4,965
1976	+ 1,132	− 5,461	− 4,329

Sources: DBS, Statistics Canada, *The Canadian Balance of International Payments — A Compendium of Statistics from 1946 to 1965; The Canadian Balance of International Payments 1966 −*.

3. Imports by Country

Year	($ Millions) Total	U.S.	Geographical Distribution (%) U.K. + W. Europe	Japan	Other
1945	1,585.7	75.8	10.1	—	14.1
1946	1,927.3	72.9	12.5	*	14.6
1947	2,573.9	76.7	9.6	*	13.7
1948	2,636.9	68.5	14.1	0.1	17.3
1949	2,761.2	70.7	14.2	0.2	14.9
1950	3,174.2	67.1	16.0	0.3	16.6
1951	4,084.0	68.8	14.7	0.2	16.3
1952	4,030.4	73.9	12.7	0.3	13.1
1953	4,382.8	73.5	14.3	0.3	11.9
1954	4,093.1	72.3	14.0	0.4	13.3
1955	4,712.3	73.3	12.8	0.7	13.2
1956	5,705.4	72.9	13.7	1.0	12.4
1957	5,623.4	71.1	14.9	1.0	13.0
1958	5,050.4	68.5	16.3	1.3	13.9
1959	5,508.9	67.3	17.3	1.8	13.6
1960	5,482.6	67.2	17.5	2.0	13.3
1961	5,768.5	67.0	17.9	2.0	13.1
1962	6,257.7	68.7	16.1	2.0	13.2
1963	6,558.2	67.8	15.3	1.9	15.0
1964	7,487.7	69.0	15.2	2.3	13.5
1965	8,633.1	70.0	15.4	2.6	12.0
1966	9,866.4	72.3	14.4	2.5	10.8
1967	11,075.1	72.4	14.1	2.7	10.8
1968	12,357.9	73.2	13.3	2.9	10.6
1969	14,201.6	72.5	13.6	3.4	10.5
1970	13,951.9	71.1	13.9	4.1	10.9
1971	15,606.5	70.1	14.0	5.1	10.8
1972	18,669.4	69.0	14.0	5.7	11.3
1973	23,325.3	70.8	13.0	4.3	11.9
1974	31,692.1	67.3	11.8	4.5	16.4
1975	34,635.5	68.0	11.8	3.4	16.8
1976	37,432.6	68.6	10.7	4.1	16.6

*Less than 0.1%.

4. Exports by Country

Year	($ Millions) Total	U.S.	U.K. + W. Europe	Japan	Other
1945	3,218.3	37.2	42.5	–	20.3
1946	2,312.2	38.4	40.3	*	21.3
1947	2,774.9	37.3	40.5	*	22.2
1948	3,075.0	48.8	33.0	0.2	21.0
1949	2,992.9	50.2	31.7	0.1	18.0
1950	3,118.3	64.8	21.8	0.6	12.8
1951	3,914.4	58.7	25.5	1.8	14.0
1952	4,301.0	53.6	28.9	2.3	15.2
1953	4,117.4	58.7	25.6	2.8	12.9
1954	3,881.2	59.7	25.9	2.4	12.0
1955	4,281.7	59.8	27.2	2.1	10.9
1956	4,789.7	58.8	28.3	2.6	10.3
1957	4,839.0	59.3	26.8	2.8	11.1
1958	4,791.4	58.6	27.6	2.1	11.7
1959	5,021.6	61.4	24.7	2.7	11.2
1960	5,255.5	55.7	28.7	3.4	12.2
1961	5,754.9	54.0	26.7	4.0	15.3
1962	6,798.5	58.4	24.8	3.4	13.4
1963	6,178.5	55.4	24.5	4.3	15.8
1964	8,094.2	52.8	24.2	4.0	19.0
1965	8,525.0	56.8	23.9	3.7	15.6
1966	10,325.3	59.9	20.2	3.9	16.0
1967	11,419.9	63.7	18.7	5.1	12.5
1968	13,605.0	67.3	16.8	4.5	11.4
1969	14,869.1	70.7	15.4	4.3	9.6
1970	16,401.0	64.4	18.6	4.9	12.1
1971	17,320.8	67.2	16.4	4.6	11.8
1972	20,149.9	69.0	14.5	4.7	11.8
1973	25,419.6	67.2	14.4	7.1	11.3
1974	32,176.5	66.2	14.7	6.9	12.2
1975	33,104.2	65.4	14.4	6.4	13.8
1976	37,258.8	68.4	13.5	6.4	11.7

*Less than 0.1%
Sources: *Canada Year Book 1945-*; Statistics Canada, *Exports*; Statistics Canada, *Imports*.

5. Unemployment

Year (31 March)	Labour Force ('000)	Unemployed ('000)	% Unemployed
1945	4,520	73	1.6
1946	4,862	124	2.5
1947	4,954	921	1.8
1948	5,035	81	1.6
1949	5,092	101	1.9
1950	5,198	142	2.7
1951	5,236	81	1.5
1952	5,344	105	1.9
1953	5,246	213	4.0
1954	5,343	346	6.4
1955	5,447	421	7.7
1956	5,605	321	5.7
1957	5,809	378	6.5
1958	6,006	636	10.5
1959	6,091	553	9.0
1960	6,244	607	9.7
1961	6,357	702	11.0
1962	6,460	559	8.6
1963	6,523	550	8.4
1964	6,742	456	6.7
1965	6,908	387	5.6
1966	7,162	341	4.7
1967	7,489	400	5.3
1968	7,608	488	6.4
1969	7,919	448	5.6
1970	8,067	542	6.7
1971	8,336	650	7.7
1972	8,658	642	7.4
1973	8,996	608	6.7
1974	9,331	599	6.4
1975	9,679	739	7.6
1976	10,019	759	7.6

Source: DBS, Statistics Canada, *The Labour Force.*

6. Foreign Exchange Value of the Canadian Dollar

Year End	U.S. Dollar	Cost of (in $ Canadian) British Pound	Japanese Yen
1945	1.10	4.43	
1946	1.00	4.02	
1947	1.00	4.02	
1948	1.00	4.02	
1949	1.10	3.0725	
1950	1.0621	2.9663	
1951	1.0119	2.8138	
1952	.9703	2.7256	
1953	.9738	2.7363	
1954	.9657	2.69	
1955	.9991	2.8009	
1956	.9597	2.6744	
1957	.9841	2.7650	
1958	.9644	2.7028	
1959	.9522	2.6658	
1960	.9966	2.7934	
1961	1.0434	2.9300	
1962	1.0772	3.0190	
1963	1.0806	3.0221	
1964	1.0738	2.9958	
1965	1.0750	3.0143	.002995
1966	1.0838	3.0090	.002975
1967	1.0806	2.9658	.002979
1968	1.0728	2.5794	.002989
1969	1.0728	2.5739	.003005
1970	1.0113	2.5016	.002916
1971	1.0022	2.4687	.002912
1972	.995	2.4797	.003270
1973	.995	2.3092	.003553
1974	.99	2.3233	.003300
1975	1.015	2.0564	.003331
1976	1.013	1.7165	.003457

Sources: Bank of Canada, *Currency Bulletin*, 1973, 1974, 1975; Statistics Canada, *Canada's International Investment Position 1945–1965; The Canadian Balance of International Payments 1965–1972.*

7. Foreign Investment in Canada

Total Foreign Long-Term Investment by Source

Year	Total ($ Million)	Distribution (%) U.S.	U.K.	Other
1945	7,092	70.3	24.6	5.1
1946	7,178	71.8	23.2	5.0
1947	7,174	71.8	22.7	5.5
1948	7,491	74.3	21.2	4.5
1949	7,960	74.1	21.5	4.4
1950	8,664	75.5	20.1	4.4
1951	9,477	76.8	18.8	4.4
1952	10,384	77.0	18.1	4.9
1953	11,461	77.3	17.5	5.2
1954	12,554	77.0	17.3	5.7
1955	13,473	76.2	17.4	6.4
1956	15,569	75.7	17.1	7.2
1957	17,464	75.9	16.7	7.4
1958	19,010	75.9	16.2	7.9
1959	20,857	75.8	15.3	8.9
1960	22,214	75.2	15.1	9.7
1961	23,606	76.2	14.3	9.5
1962	24,889	76.9	13.6	9.5
1963	26,205	78.3	12.7	9.0
1964	27,474	78.4	12.5	9.1
1965	29,603	79.0	11.8	9.2
1966	32,090	80.1	10.9	9.0
1967	34,702	80.7	10.3	9.0
1968	37,979	80.3	9.7	10.0
1969	41,602	79.4	9.1	11.5
1970	44,037	79.2	9.1	11.7
1971	46,250	78.5	9.3	12.1
1972	49,933	77.2	9.1	13.6

Source: *Canada Year Book 1946—*; Statistics Canada.

Foreign Ownership by Sector

Abbreviations:
n.a.—not available
x—confidential
Unclassified—corporations not required to report under Corporations
and Labour Unions Returns Act (CALURA)

		Degree of Foreign Ownership (Expressed as % of Total Assets of All Corporations in Sector)			
Sector	Year	50-100%	40-49%	Govt. Ownership	Unclassified
Agriculture	1965	9	47		45
Forestry	1966	8	53		39
Fishing	1967	14	49	—	37
	1968	13	52	—	35
	1969	16	52	—	32
	1970	13	54	—	33
	1971	13	57	x	x
	1972	11	61	x	x
	1973	11	64	—	25
Mining	1965	58	40		2
	1966	58	41		2
	1967	58	39	1	2
	1968	60	37	1	2
	1969	65	33	1	1
	1970	63	35	1	1
	1971	63	35	1	1
	1972	64	34	1	1
	1973	54	44	1	1
Manufacturing	1965	55	40	—	5
	1966	56	40	—	4
	1967	57	39	1	3
	1968	58	38	1	3
	1969	58	39	1	2
	1970	58	38	1	2
	1971	58	39	1	2
	1972	56	41	1	2
	1973	57	40	1	2
Construction	1965	10	69	—	21
	1966	13	70	—	17
	1967	14	69	x	x
	1968	14	68	x	x
	1969	11	72	x	x

continued

Sector	Year	Degree of Foreign Ownership (Expressed as % of Total Assets of All Corporations in Sector)			
		50-100%	40-49%	Govt. Ownership	Unclassified
	1970	15	68	x	x
	1971	17	68	x	x
	1972	13	73	—	14
	1973	12	75	—	13
Utilities	1965	7	29		64
	1966	7	28		66
	1967	4	36	59	1
	1968	5	35	59	1
	1969	5	36	58	1
	1970	5	36	58	1
	1971	5	36	57	1
	1972	6	36	57	1
	1973	6	36	57	1
Wholesale Trade	1965	27	60	n.a.	13
	1966	28	60	n.a.	12
	1967	25	56	x	x
	1968	28	54	9	9
	1969	27	53	10	10
	1970	27	55	x	x
	1971	31	53	7	8
	1972	30	57	6	7
	1973	30	58	6	6
Retail Trade	1965	18	56	n.a.	26
	1966	19	58	n.a.	23
	1967	20	56	2	22
	1968	21	56	2	21
	1969	21	56	2	21
	1970	22	55	2	22
	1971	22	56	2	20
	1972	22	58	2	18
	1973	21	59	2	17
Services	1965	13	52	n.a.	35
	1966	16	54	n.a.	31
	1967	18	53	x	x
	1968	20	53	x	x
	1969	23	52	x	x
	1970	22	53	x	x
	1971	23	54	x	x
	1972	21	58	x	x
	1973	22	58	1	18

continued

Sector	Year	Degree of Foreign Ownership (Expressed as % of Total Assets of All Corporations in Sector)			
		50-100%	40-49%	Govt. Ownership	Unclassified
Total	1965	11	34	n.a.	54
All	1966	12	35	n.a.	53
Industries	1967	12	35	n.a.	53
	1968	13	34	n.a.	53
	1969	12	34	n.a.	54
	1970	12	33	x	x
	1971	12	32	6	49
	1972	10	31	9	50
	1973	12	30	8	50
Total	1965	36	43	18	3
Non-Financial	1966	37	43	18	2
Industries	1967	33	47	19	6
	1968	34	42	18	6
	1969	34	42	18	6
	1970	34	42	18	6
	1971	35	42	18	5
	1972	33	44	18	5
	1973	33	45	17	5

Source: DBS, Statistics Canada, Corporations and Labour Unions Returns Act, Part I: Corporations 1965—.

Foreign Control by Sector

Abbreviations:
x—confidential
Unclassified—corporations not required to report under CALURA

Sector	Year	Country of Control (Expressed as % of Total Assets of All Corporations in Sector)				
		U.S.	Other	Cdn. Private	Cdn. Public	Unclassified
Agriculture	1968	11	1	53	—	35
Fishing	1969	10	5	53	—	32
Forestry	1970	9	4	54	—	33
	1971	8	4	57	x	x
	1972	6	5	61	x	x
	1973	6	4	64	—	25

continued

Sector	Year	Country of Control (Expressed as % of Total Assets of All Corporations in Sector)				
		U.S.	Other	Cdn. Private	Cdn. Public	Unclassified
Mining	1968	52	12	33	1	2
	1969	57	11	30	1	1
	1970	58	11	28	1	1
	1971	59	10	29	1	1
	1972	50	10	38	1	1
	1973	48	10	40	1	1
Manufacturing	1968	45	13	38	1	3
	1969	45	13	39	1	2
	1970	44	15	37	1	2
	1971	44	15	38	1	2
	1972	42	15	41	1	2
	1973	42	15	41	1	2
Construction	1968	9	6	67	x	x
	1969	7	5	71	x	x
	1970	8	9	67	x	x
	1971	8	10	67	x	x
	1972	6	9	71	—	14
	1973	5	9	73	—	13
Utilities	1968	7	1	33	58	1
	1969	7	1	33	58	1
	1970	8	1	32	58	1
	1971	7	2	32	57	1
	1972	8	2	31	57	1
	1973	8	2	32	57	1
Wholesale Trade	1968	17	11	54	9	9
	1969	15	11	54	10	10
	1970	15	13	54	x	x
	1971	15	18	52	7	8
	1972	16	16	54	6	7
	1973	15	16	56	6	6
Retail Trade	1968	16	4	57	2	21
	1969	17	4	56	2	21
	1970	14	8	54	2	22
	1971	14	8	55	2	20
	1972	14	8	57	2	18
	1973	13	6	62	2	12
Services	1968	15	5	53	x	x
	1969	18	5	52	x	x

continued

Sector	Year	Country of Control (Expressed as % of Total Assets of All Corporations in Sector)				
		U.S.	Other	Cdn. Private	Cdn. Public	Unclassified
	1970	18	5	52	x	x
	1971	18	5	53	x	x
	1972	17	5	57	x	x
	1973	17	6	58	1	18
Total,	1968	28	8	40	18	6
Non-	1969	28	8	40	18	6
Financial	1970	28	9	40	18	6
Industries	1971	27	10	40	18	5
	1972	25	10	43	18	5
	1973	25	9	44	17	5

Note: Because of rounding figures may not add to exactly 100%.
Source: DBS, Statistics Canada, Corporations and Labour Unions Returns Act, Part I: Corporations 1965—.

8. Consumer Price Index (1971 = 100)

Year*		Year*	
1945	43.2	1962	75.3
1946	43.6	1963	76.6
1947	46.2	1964	77.9
1948	53.8	1965	79.5
1949	57.9	1966	81.9
1950	58.1	1967	84.7
1951	62.5	1968	88.5
1952	68.6	1969	91.9
1953	67.2	1970	96.1
1954	67.2	1971	97.7
1955	67.5	1972	102.5
1956	67.8	1973	108.3
1957	69.8	1974	118.1
1958	71.6	1975	132.4
1959	73.2	1976	145.1
1960	74.0	1977	154.0
1961	75.0		

* As of January each year.
Source: Statistics Canada, Consumer Price Indexes for Canada, Cansim D616101.

9. Trade Union Membership in Canada

Year	Total Membership ('000)	Proportion of Civilian Labour Force (%)
1945	711	15.7
1950	1,006	19.3
1955	1,268	23.6
1960	1,459	23.5
1965	1,589	23.2
1970	2,112	27.2
1975	2,875	29.7

10. Trade Union Membership by Congress Affiliation

Abbreviations:
TLC—Trades and Labour Congress
CCL—Canadian Congress of Labour
CLC—Canadian Labour Congress
CCCL—Canadian and Catholic Confederation of Labour
CNTU—Confederation of National Trade Unions (since 1964)

Year	TLC No. ('000)	%*	CCL No. ('000)	%*	CLC[1] No. ('000)	%*	CCCL/CNTU No. ('000)	%*	Unaffiliated or Other No. ('000)	%*
1945	312	43.9	245	34.4			68	9.6	85	12.0
1950	459	45.7	302	30.0			80	8.0	163	16.3
1955	601	47.4	361	28.5			100	7.9	206	16.2
1960					1,123	77.0	102	7.0	234	16.2
1965					1,181	74.4	150	9.4	258	16.3
1970					1,632	75.1	207	9.5	333	15.4
1975					2,043	71.1	173	6.0	657	22.9

* Of total union membership.
[1] CLC formed by merger of TLC and CCL in 1956.

11. Canada's Ten Largest Unions: 1945–1975

1945	1950	1955	1960	1965	1970	1975
Auto Workers 51,000	Auto Workers 60,000	Steelworkers 60,000	Steelworkers 82,000	Steelworkers 11,000	Steelworkers 150,000	Public Employees (CUPE) 198,000
Steelworkers 30,000	Steelworkers 50,000	Auto Workers 60,000	Carpenters 66,134	Public Employees (CUPE) 84,800	Public Employees (CUPE) 136,127	Steelworkers 186,996
Cdn. Brotherhood of Railway Trainmen* 28,000	Carpenters 37,210	Carpenters 54,709	Auto Workers 60,968	Auto Workers 77,500	Public Service Alliance 119,743	Public Service Alliance 135,998
Machinists 26,000	Railway Trainmen (CBRT)* 32,500	Machinists 49,097	Public Employees (CUPE) 44,873	Carpenters 64,000	Auto Workers 109,274	Auto Workers 117,486
Mineworkers 23,710	Pulp and Sulphite Workers 28,000	Woodworkers 33,881	Machinists 39,943	Woodworkers 43,600	Carpenters 72,209	Carpenters 89,010
Carpenters 20,271	Machinists 26,686	Railway Trainmen (CBRT)* 33,851	Teamsters 39,676	Teamsters 42,400	Teamsters 58,178	Corporation des Enseignants du Québec 84,905
Brotherhood of Railway Trainmen* 18,811	Mineworkers 25,124	Mine, Mill and Smelter Workers 32,000	Electrical Workers 36,733	Machinists 41,200	Electrical Workers 56,918	Teamsters 75,638
Maintenance of Way Employees 18,187	Mine, Mill and Smelter Workers 25,000	Pulp and Sulphite Workers 31,957	Woodworkers 36,688	Electrical Workers 38,000	Machinists 53,003	Electrical Workers 63,463
Railway Carmen 16,079	Maintenance of Way Employees 24,201	Railway Carmen 26,356	Pulp and Sulphite Workers 25,235	Pulp and Sulphite Workers 36,900	Fédération National des Services 49,362	Fédération des Affaires Sociales 61,130
Nat. Federation of Building Unions 15,404	Electrical Workers 22,857	Mineworkers 23,750	Railway Trainmen (CBRT)* 33,150	Railway Trainmen (CBRT)* 32,100	Woodworkers 48,904	Machinists 57,209

*Canadian Brotherhood of Railway Trainmen (CBRT) is a national union; Brotherhood of Railway Trainmen an international union. Both serve essentially the same occupational group.

12. Proportion of Canadian Union Membership in International Unions

Year	Total Membership in All Unions No. ('000)	Membership in International Unions No. ('000)	%
1945	711	471	66.2
1950	1,006	713	70.9
1955	1,268	894	70.5
1960	1,459	1,052	72.1
1965	1,589	1,125	70.8
1970	2,112	1,359	62.5
1975	2,875	1,479	51.4

Source: (Tables 9–12) Canada, Department of Labour, *Labour Organizations in Canada*.

VIII
POPULATION AND LANGUAGE

1. Population by Region

Region	1941		1951		Year 1961		1971		1975	
	No. ('000)	%	No. ('000)	%	No. ('000)	%	No. ('000)	%	No. ('000)	%
Atlantic	1,130	9.8	1,618	11.5	1,898	10.4	2,058	9.5	2,165	9.5
Quebec	3,332	29.0	4,056	28.9	5,259	28.8	6,028	27.9	6,188	27.1
Ontario	3,788	32.9	4,598	32.8	6,236	34.2	7,703	35.7	8,226	36.1
West (Incl. Territories)	3,257	28.3	3,739	26.7	4,846	26.6	5,780	26.8	6,221	27.3
Total	11,507	100.0*	14,009	100.0*	18,238	100.0*	21,568	100.0*	22,800	100.0*

*May not total 100.0 due to rounding.
Note: As of 1 June each year; 1941–1971 figures from Statistics Canada, *Censuses of Canada*; 1975 figures from Statistics Canada, *Estimated Population of Canada by Province*, 1975.

2. Population by Province

Province	1941		1951		Year 1961		1971		1975	
	No. ('000)	%	No. ('000)	%	No. ('000)	%	No. ('000)	%	No. ('000)	%
Nfld.			361	2.6	458	2.5	522	2.4	549	2.4
P.E.I.	95	0.8	98	0.7	105	0.6	112	0.5	119	0.5
N.S.	578	5.0	643	4.6	737	4.0	789	3.7	822	3.6
N.B.	457	4.0	516	3.7	598	3.3	635	2.9	675	2.9
P.Q.	3,332	29.0	4,056	28.9	5,259	28.8	6,028	27.9	6,188	27.1
Ont.	3,788	32.9	4,598	32.8	6,236	34.2	7,703	35.7	8,226	36.1
Man.	730	6.3	777	5.5	922	5.1	988	4.6	1,019	4.5
Sask.	896	7.8	832	5.9	925	5.1	926	4.3	918	4.0
Alta.	796	6.9	940	6.7	1,332	7.3	1,628	7.5	1,768	7.8

B.C.	818	7.1	1,165	8.3	1,629	8.9	2,185	10.1	2,457	10.8
Total	11,507	100.0*	14,009	100.0*	18,238	100.0*	21,568	100.0*	22,800	100.0*

*May not total 100.0 due to rounding

Notes: As of 1 June of each year; 1941–1971 figures from Statistics Canada, *Censuses of Canada*; 1975 figures from Statistics Canada, *Estimated Population of Canada by Province*, 1975.

As of June 1975 estimated population of territories as follows:

Yukon — 21,000

N.W.T. — 38,000.

3. Population by Ethnic Origin

Ethnic Origin	Year							
	1941		1951		1961		1971	
	No. ('000)	%	No. ('000)	%	No. ('000)	%	No. ('000)	%
British	5,716	49.7	6,710	47.9	7,997	43.8	9,624	44.6
French	3,483	30.3	4,319	30.8	5,540	30.4	6,180	28.7
German	465	4.0	620	4.4	1,050	5.8	1,317	6.1
Italian	113	1.0	152	1.1	450	2.5	731	3.4
Jewish	170	1.5	182	1.3	173	1.0	297	1.4
Dutch	213	1.8	264	1.9	430	2.4	426	2.0
Polish	167	1.5	220	1.6	324	1.8	316	1.5
Scandinavian	245	2.1	283	2.0	387	2.1	385	1.8
Ukrainian	306	2.7	395	2.8	473	2.6	581	2.7
Indian & Eskimo	126	1.1	166	1.1	220	1.2	295	1.4
Others & Not Stated	504	4.3	699	5.0	1,195	6.4	1,416	6.6
Total	11,507	100	14,009	100	18,238	100	21,568	100

Source: Statistics Canada, *Censuses of Canada*.

4. Population by Mother Tongue

Mother Tongue	1941 No. ('000)	1941 %	1951 No. ('000)	1951 %	1961 No. ('000)	1961 %	1971 No. ('000)	1971 %	1971 – Habitual Use[1] No. ('000)	%
English	6,488	56.4	8,281	59.1	10,661	58.5	12,974	60.2	14,446	67.0
French	3,355	29.2	4,069	29.0	5,123	28.1	5,794	26.9	5,546	25.7
German	322	2.8	329	2.4	564	3.1	561	2.6	213	1.0
Italian	80	0.7	92	0.7	340	1.9	538	2.5	425	2.0
Dutch	53	0.5	88	0.6	170	0.9	145	0.7	36	0.2
Polish	129	1.1	129	0.9	162	0.9	135	0.6	71	0.3
Scandinavian	144	1.3	107	0.8	117	0.6	84	0.4	10	–
Ukrainian	313	2.7	352	2.5	361	2.0	310	1.4	145	0.7
Yiddish	130	1.1	104	0.7	82	0.5	50	0.2	26	0.1
Indian & Eskimo	131	1.1	145	1.0	167	0.9	180	0.8	137	0.6
Others & Not Stated	303	3.1	313	2.3	492	2.6	797	3.7	513	2.4

[1]Measures language most commonly used in the home rather than mother tongue, i.e., language first learned in childhood and still understood.

Source: Statistics Canada, *Censuses of Canada*.

5. Population by Mother Tongue and Linguistic Region,* 1941–1971 (%)

Mother Tongue	Atlantic Region	Northern New Brunswick	Northern and Eastern Quebec	Southern and Western Quebec	Eastern and Northern Ontario	Southern and Western Ontario	Western Region	Canada
1941:								
English	90	49	4	23	56	87	60	57
French	7	59	95	69	33	2	4	29
Other	3	1	1	7	11	11	36	14
1951:								
English	94	39	4	23	59	86	70	59
French	4	60	96	71	32	2	4	29
Other	1	1	1	6	9	11	26	12
1961:								
English	94	40	4	21	60	81	73	59
French	4	59	95	70	29	2	3	28
Other	2	1	1	9	11	17	24	13
1971:								
English	95	41	3	20	64	80	77	60
French	4	58	96	71	27	2	3	27
Other	1	1	1	9	9	18	20	13

*The linguistic regions are those suggested by Richard J. Joy, *Languages in Conflict*, Toronto: McClelland and Stewart, 1972, pp. 17–21.
Source: Statistics Canada, *Censuses of Canada*.

6. Degree of Assimilation to English

Distribution (%) of Population of English Mother Tongue by Ethnic Origin

Ethnic Origin	Year				1971 – Habitual Use[1]
	1941	1951	1961	1971	
British	98.3	98.7	98.6	97.7	98.4
French	5.8	7.9	10.0	10.4	14.5
German	45.3	58.2	59.0	61.7	84.3
Italian	23.7	34.3	22.2	25.1	37.2
Jewish	19.2	42.7	57.7	69.7	83.9
Dutch	61.4	57.1	51.8	61.7	89.7
Polish	14.5	28.7	40.3	52.0	75.3
Scandinavian	41.8	62.7	69.7	77.8	96.7
Ukrainian	5.1	18.6	33.9	48.5	76.1
Indian & Eskimo	8.1	15.4	26.7	40.5	53.3

[1]Measures language most commonly used in the home rather than mother tongue, i.e., language first learned in childhood and still understood.

Source: Statistics Canada, *Censuses of Canada*.

IX
MISCELLANEOUS

1. Canada: Territorial Size and Development

Date	Province(s) or Territory Created/Entering Confederation	Present Area (sq. mi.)
1 Jul 1867	Nova Scotia	28,354
	New Brunswick	21,425
	Quebec	594,860
	Ontario	412,582
15 Jul 1870	Manitoba	251,000
	Northwest Territories (Present division into Districts of Mackenzie, Keewatin, and Franklin made 1 January 1920.)	1,304,903
20 Jul 1871	British Columbia	366,255
1 Jul 1873	Prince Edward Island	2,184
13 Jun 1898	Yukon Territory	207,076
1 Sep 1905	Saskatchewan	251,700
	Alberta	255,285
31 Mar 1949	Newfoundland and Labrador	156,185
	Canada	3,851,809

Source: *Canada Year Book 1973.*

2. Direct Amendments to the British North America Act 1945–1975

Title	Subject and Section(s) If Any Concerned
B.N.A. Act 1946	Establish new rules for distribution of seats in the House of Commons among the provinces and territories. Section 51.
B.N.A. (No. 1) Act 1949	Provide for entry of Nfld. into Confederation. Sections 21,22, 28, 93.
B.N.A. (No. 2) Act 1949	Grant power to federal Parliament to amend constitution in certain areas. Section 91.
B.N.A. Act 1951	Grant power to federal Parliament to legislate with respect to old age pensions subject to provincial paramountcy. Section 94A.
B.N.A. Act 1952*	Modify rules established in 1946 (see above) for representation in House of Commons. Section 51.

continued

Title	Subject and Section(s) If Any Concerned
B.N.A. Act 1960	Institute retirement at age 75 for superior court judges. Section 99.
B.N.A. Act 1964	Enlarge powers granted to federal Parliament in 1951 to legislate with respect to old age pensions, subject still to provincial paramountcy. Section 94A.
B.N.A. Act 1965*	Provide for retirement of Senators appointed after 2 Jun 1965 at age 75. Section 29.
Representation Act 1974*	Establish new rules for distribution of seats in the House of Commons among the provinces and territories. Section 51.
B.N.A. Act 1975*	Provide for Senate representation for Yukon and Northwest Territories. Sections 21, 22, 28.
NWT Representation Act 1975*	Increase representation of Northwest Territories in House of Commons. Section 51.

* Amendment carried out by Parliament of Canada under authority of B.N.A. (No. 2) Act 1949.

3. Major Royal Commissions 1945–1976

Date Appointed	Subject
1945	Loyalty of Japanese Canadians
1946	Espionage in Public Service
	Indian Act
1948	Prices
	Transportation
1949	Arts, Letters and Sciences in Canada ("Massey Commission")
1951	South Saskatchewan River Projects
1954	Criminal Law and Sexual Psychopaths
	Criminal Law and Defence of Insanity
1955	Canada's Long-Term Economic Prospects ("Gordon Commission")
	Broadcasting ("Fowler Commission")
1957	Energy ("Borden Commission")
	Newfoundland Terms of Union
1959	Freight Rates
	Coal

continued

Date Appointed	Subject
1960	Government Organization ("Glassco Commission") Automotive Industry ("Bladen Commission") Publishing Industry ("O'Leary Commission")
1961	Unemployment Insurance Banking and Finance ("Porter Commission") Health Services ("Hall Commission")
1962	Taxation ("Carter Commission")
1963	Bilingualism and Biculturalism ("Dunton-Laurendeau Commission")
1964	Extradition of Lucien Rivard ("Dorion Commission")
1966	Mr. Justice Landreville Gerda Munsinger ("Spence Commission") Canadian Security
1967	Status of Women
1969	Non-Medical Use of Drugs ("LeDain Commission") Prices and Incomes Indian Treaties
1974	Environmental and Socio-Economic Implications of a Mackenzie Valley Pipeline ("Berger Commission")
1975	Concentration of Corporate Power in Canada
1976	Use of French in Air Traffic Control Financial Organization and Accountability in Federal Government

Sources: *Canada Year Book 1945 –*; *Canadian News Facts 1976.*

4. Commonwealth Heads of Government Meetings

Date	Place
4–13 Apr 1945	London
23 Apr–23 May 1946	London
11–22 Oct 1948	London
21–28 Apr 1949	London
4–12 Jan 1951	London
3–9 Jun 1953	London
31 Jan–8 Feb 1955	London
27 Jun–6 Jul 1956	London
26 Jun–5 Jul 1957	London
3–13 May 1960	London

continued

Date	Place
8−17 Mar 1961	London
10−19 Sep 1962	London
8−13 Jul 1964	London
17−25 Jan 1965	London
11−12 Jan 1966	Lagos
6−15 Sep 1966	London
7−10 Jan 1969	London
14−22 Jan 1971	Singapore
2−10 Aug 1973	Ottawa
28 Apr−6 May 1975	Kingston, Jamaica

Source: *Canada Year Book 1945−*.

5. Major International Agreements Entered into by Canada 1945−1976

Agreement	Date Signed by Canada
Agreements Concerning United Nations and Other International Organizations	
United Nations Charter	26 Jun 1945
Constitution of the Food and Agriculture Organization (FAO) of the U.N.	16 Oct 1945
Final Act of the U.N. Conference for the establishment of an Educational, Scientific and Cultural Organization (UNESCO)	16 Nov 1945
Constitution of the International Labour Organization (ILO)	9 Oct 1946
Constitution of the International Refugee Organization (UNRRA)	15 Dec 1946
Universal Postal Convention	5 Jul 1947
Inter-American Telecommunications Convention	27 Sep 1947
International Telecommunications Convention	2 Oct 1947
Convention of the World Meteorological Organization	11 Oct 1947
Universal Copyright Convention	6 Sep 1952
Statute of the International Convention	26 Oct 1956
U.N-Canada agreement establishing United Nations Emergency Force (UNEF) in the Middle East (deemed to have taken effect 13 Nov 1956)	Jun 21/Jul 29, 1957
Convention on the Organization for Economic Co-operation and Development (OECD)	14 Dec 1960
Agreement establishing the Asian Development Bank	4 Dec 1965

continued

Agreement	Date Signed by Canada
Agreement establishing the Caribbean Development Bank	18 Oct 1969
Acceptance by Canada of the compulsory jurisdiction of the International Court of Justice	7 Apr 1970
Agreement relating to the International Telecommunications Satellite Organization (Intelsat)	20 Aug 1971

Canada-U.S. Agreements

Agreement on arbitration of environment damages caused by Trail (B.C.) Smelter	17 Nov 1949
Agreement to establish continental radar system for air defence	1 Aug 1951
Agreement to construct St. Lawrence Seaway	30 Jun 1952
Agreement establishing North American Air Defence Command (NORAD)	12 May 1958
Agreement for Canadian participation in Ballistic Missile Early Warning System (BMEWS)	13 Jul 1959
Columbia River Treaty	17 Jan 1961
Agreement concerning supply of F-101 and F-104 aircraft to Canada	12 Jun 1961
Agreement for Canadian acceptance of BOMARC anti-aircraft missiles	27 Sep 1961
Canada-U.S. Automotive Agreement	17 Jan 1965
Extension of NORAD agreement for five years	30 Mar 1968
Agreement on Great Lakes Water Quality	15 Apr 1972
Extension of NORAD agreement for two years	10 May 1973
Extension of NORAD agreement for five years	8 May 1975

Other Agreements

Acts of German Military Surrender	Apr 29/May 4, 7, 9, 1945
Instrument of Japan's Surrender	2 Sep 1945
Canada-U.K.-U.S. Declaration on Atomic Energy	15 Nov 1945
Treaty of Peace with Italy	10 Feb 1947
Treaty of Peace with Hungary	10 Feb 1947
Treaty of Peace with Romania	10 Feb 1947
Treaty of Peace with Finland	10 Feb 1947
General Agreement on Tariffs and Trade (GATT)	30 Oct 1947
North Atlantic Treaty (establishing NATO)	3 May 1949
Convention on the Prevention and Punishment of the Crime of Genocide	28 Nov 1949
International Convention for the Northwest Atlantic Fisheries (ICNAF)	3 Jul 1950
Termination of State of War with Germany (by Royal Proclamation)	10 Jul 1951
Treaty of Peace with Japan	8 Sep 1951

continued

Agreement	Date Signed by Canada
Accession of Greece and Turkey to NATO	17 Oct 1951
Accession of Federal Republic of Germany to NATO	29 Apr 1955
Austrian State Treaty	15 May 1955
Law of the Sea — Convention on the Continental Shelf	29 Apr 1958
Declaration on the Neutrality of Laos	23 Jul 1962
Nuclear Test Ban Treaty	8 Aug 1963
Canada-India agreement on the Rajasthan Atomic Power Station	16 Dec 1963
Canada-France agreement on provincial "ententes" with foreign governments	17 Nov 1965
Nuclear Non-Proliferation Treaty	Jul 23/29, 1968
Convention for Suppressing Aircraft Hijacking	16 Dec 1970
Treaty Prohibiting Nuclear Weapons on the Seabed	11 Feb 1971
Act of the International Conference on Vietnam	2 Mar 1973
Canada-Norway Fisheries Agreement	2 Dec 1975
Canada-USSR Fisheries Agreement	22 Dec 1975/19 May 1976
Canada-South Korea Agreement on Atomic Energy	26 Jan 1976
Canada-Argentina Agreement on Atomic Energy	30 Jan 1976
Framework Agreement for Commercial and Co-operation between Canada and the European Communities	6 Jul 1976

Source: Canada, Department of External Affairs, *Treaty Series*, 1945–1976.